FOOD STAMPS TO FRANCHISE

A Publication of *Tall Pine Books*
119 E Center Street, Suite B4A | Warsaw, Indiana 46580
www.tallpinebooks.com

| 1 23 23 20 16 02 |

Published in the United States of America

FOOD STAMPS
TO FRANCHISE

A LIFE JOURNEY FROM BROKENNESS TO SUCCESS

CHRIS MCMURRAY

This work is deducted to the most steadfast and inspirational person I know, my wife Kelly. Without her, and her consistent surrender of what was comfortable, I would not be what I am today. Thank you for letting me live the adventure, I wouldn't want to be on this journey with anyone else.

CONTENTS

INTRODUCTION

M Y PALMS WERE sweaty as I worked to control my trembling. My two girls looked on as the sixteen-year-old kid hooked me into the harness that would secure me as I made my way 50 feet into the air. I was on a metal apparatus known to most people as a "ropes course."

I had never been on one before, but I thought it looked like something that I could tackle easily enough. I wanted to show my family what it meant to live life to the fullest and to see the view of the world from high in the air. In fact, I felt duty-bound to do this. With each click of the clasps, I tempered my terrified posture and felt the overwhelming sensation that I *had* to conquer this thing.

It was wintertime in Pigeon Forge, Tennessee. Snow was spitting outside, leaving millions of friendly vacationers with fewer options for outdoor activities, making indoor activities a popular choice. Wonderworks was very busy that day; we had waited almost an hour before we reached the capsule where they would weigh us and choose our harness and materials. As if trying to torture me, there were signs all along the waiting route with riveting facts about the course we were slated to tackle. One read, "The tallest course in the world, scaling more than four and a half stories in the air."

Finally I was urged to make my way over and take the first step up into the course. I went quickly as the large crowd watched. I was connected to the overhead rope first. Next, my two girls, who were seven and eight years old at the time, were strapped in, and lastly, my wife, Kelly, bravely hiding her hesitation, was also connected to the rig.

I made it to the first platform, about ten feet up and had no choice but to advance to another set of steps that would put us about mid-way to the 50-foot peak. We worked our way up, realizing we would have to coerce our overhead rope along as we advanced in the course. It was irritating to keep up with, but a better alternative than the severe ramifications of adventuring that high without that safety tool.

As we reached the peak, my confidence was growing and I became more sure of my ability to navigate the course without interruption until I came to the top. Once we reached the max height of the course there were no more stairs and we had to make our way between small platforms with tricky steps, mostly suspended between ropes. I looked out and the daunting path ahead was a series of 6 inch suspended square platforms, saddled between two skimpy looking ropes.

I felt the familiar fear sweep over me again. While I had grown in my confidence to successfully complete the course when the steps were more sure, I was very hesitant to step out onto something that seemed so unknown. I looked at the square then down to the floor 40 feet below and saw a crowd of people looking as I began to impede the flow of traffic behind me. I looked back at Kelly, and then my girls. They were puzzled. Truth is, they had not seen me like this before. I was usually the adventurer, the one to step out even when it seemed risky, but I had underestimated the fear that would overtake me at that height.

Kelly assured me that no one would hold me at fault if we needed to turn around and begin a shameful descent without experiencing any of the ropes course. To me that simply wasn't an option. Not to mention, that would force about twenty others to back-track down to the bottom so I could exit. The only path forward was to step out onto that small block, even if everything in me wanted to retreat. It was a step of faith—believing in the assurances of the one who had made the apparatus.

There was no time left.

Leading the pack, my family began to cheer for me from behind. I had to show them, in a very literal sense, what it means to step out into the unknown—and, *I did it.* I placed a foot onto the wobbly block and onto the next one, and the next. I grew slightly more comfortable with each step, but still not entirely free from subtle pangs and rushes of fear. Eventually I was able to effectively reach back and offer a helping hand to my older daughter, allowing her to step out with a little more confidence. Then she offered a hand to our younger daughter, and the same to Kelly. Suddenly there we were, on 6-inch square blocks, with nothing holding us but thin rope, all holding hands, and suspended 50 feet in the air.

Onlookers were so thrilled that we had stepped out that a loud applause erupted from below as so many were keeping up with our progress on the course. After that initial step, each one became easier and easier. Pretty soon all four of us were making our way around the top of that course, high in the air with ease.

The view and experience was incredible. I took many opportunities to stop and look down, to see all of the cool things we had read about during our wait in line. I could not help but think about all that I would have missed had I made the decision to descend back down to the start succumbing to the fear of failure that I had experienced in such a real way in the beginning.

It took me stepping out onto that square to set the pace for my family, to show them a very tangible example of what it meant to live by faith. We may find success, we may face failure, but either way, stepping out is not optional. You and I cannot escape the biblical mandate to reach beyond where we are into the great unknown.

Remember when Jesus came to the disciples walking on the water? In the gospel of Matthew I find some of the most insightful words spoken in the presence of Jesus as Peter longingly looked out onto the dark waters of the deep. As the soft reflection of light from their torches bounced off the choppy waters, Peter said, *"Lord, if it's you, tell me to come to you on the water" (Matthew 14:28).* This moment demonstrated that Peter had an eager desire to see and know what would come of his faith and destiny. He wanted to have the faith to step out and walk on the water just as Jesus did.

Peter, with his usual enthusiasm, longed to have the faith to join the Master on the water. He dropped his legs over the stern, dipped his toes into the cool water, and found success in his first steps on the lake—though, it was a short-lived stroll on liquid. When he looked around and saw the wind and waves, he allowed the fear of failure to overtake him. He found himself up to his ankles, knees, and hips in water, sinking quickly and in sincere need of rescue. Jesus reached out and offered a helping hand to bring Peter out of the water, pulling him up from his own fears.

In that moment Jesus had effectively shifted Peter's failure into a success, even in the presence of the 11 unwilling participants who were looking on from the boat. I find this to mimic common trends in our current culture. Most look on, waiting to laugh and point fingers at the one that steps out. But the reward is much greater for those willing to step out, as opposed to those that refuse to take the risk. It's been said that it's better to be a wet water-walker than a dry boat-dweller. Most would have viewed Peter's exercise as an abject failure, but the faith that would be developed in Peter stepping out would set him up for even greater impact as his ministry would expand in the years to come.

The lesson is this: sometimes we have to experience failure to get us to the ultimate success that God is calling us to. Failure is not a final stop but a building block. Ultimate success is not reached through many successes, but often...many failures. Our story exemplifies many of these realities, and I pray it brings you hope so that you too can rise above where you are and learn from those dark places of failure. I pray you find the courage to faithfully step out into your God-given destiny. Stepping out and failing is only temporary. Staying where you are and never moving forward is permanent. Which price are you willing to pay?

If I were being completely honest, some of what we will explore throughout the course of this book has been painful to relive. Though, I am certain that you can find the joy and success of starting something new and overcoming failure through the lessons in it. I believe we can learn from one another and there is something beautiful about the people of God gleaning wisdom from our separate, yet connected experiences on earth. As I share our experience from nothing to something, less to more, and as you hear how we overcame many obstacles to find success, I hope you find nuggets of wisdom that will help you avoid making the same costly mistakes that we did on our journey. My hope is that you will hear me, and the Lord, saying that you *can* do it. The time to step out is now.

I can tell you with certainty if God can use a radically simple-minded, common sense boy from Southwest Virginia, He can use you. We must train ourselves to shift our focus off of the things that stop us from moving forward into our God-given mission. We have to learn to temper our fear of failure long enough to step out to see the truly limitless capacity of the Lord. Along the way I will share some of my personal business insight that will help you in finding your place as you do big things for God and His mission.

This is the story of how we overcame our obstacles and found success; the story of how we went from *food stamps to franchise*, and how you, too, can find your triumph along the way.

CHAPTER ONE

ENVIRONMENT OF ENTREPRENEURSHIP

I HAVE ALWAYS loved business, even when it didn't love me back. Anyone who's been bit by the entrepreneurial bug knows that dynamic all too well. I have seen both success and failure, experiencing the latter more often than not. However, when things were good, they were *really* good and when things were bad, it was simply a learning experience, a stepping stone. This can only mean one thing: you may fail more than you succeed and still end up a success. This may seem counterintuitive, but it's a tried and true concept, proven throughout the centuries.

Even among venture capitalists, the numbers are quite interesting. The common rule of thumb is that of 10 start-ups, three or four will fail completely. Another three or four will return the original investment with no profit, and only one or two will produce substantial returns. However, those "substantial returns" are generally enough to completely cancel out and surpass the losses. This book is not a roadmap for constant success. It's a roadmap for finding the *right kind* of success *despite* some simultaneous failures.

I must confess up front that I am by no means a perfect businessman nor do I write from the perspective of some flawless mogul. I have learned primarily from the school of hard knocks and it was through failures and detours that my desire and passion grew. In many ways my entrepreneurial life has informed my spiritual life, and my spiritual life has informed my business life. Blending church and business isn't easy, but it is necessary for improving effectiveness and productivity. I am convinced that Jesus understood the full necessity of both, He was, after all, the son of a self-employed businessman.

I can relate to His astute ability to work within His father's trade. We see in Matthew 13:54-55, *"Coming to his hometown, he began teaching the people in their synagogue, and they were amazed. 'Where did this man get this wisdom and these miraculous powers?' they asked. 'Isn't this the carpenter's son? Isn't his mother's name Mary, and aren't his brothers James, Joseph, Simon and Judas?'"* (Matthew 13:54-55). Like Jesus, I experienced the pain of my abilities going unrecognized. In fact, to grasp where I am today, I'd like to give you a sketch of the upbringing that brought me here.

My dad had always been a serial entrepreneur and found success in one main area while chasing other dreams on the side. He was an early franchisee in the bustling, and highly competitive gas business. After a couple of failures, he happened upon a great location and empowered by the Exxon brand, he began to make a good living. He found himself located right in the middle of what most business leaders would call *the sweet spot*. This is the spot where you have the freedom financially to live and do what you want while running in the lane of something you love.

The business model itself combined fuel sales and car repair. I recall my dad telling me stories of how customers would come in from a walk to the station in need of a tire plug. He would literally close up the shop, run down the road to tow in the customer's car, and bring it back to repair it himself, hoping that no one would pull in needing gas in the meantime.

Dad ran his gas prices at 2 to 3 cents lower than cost to keep people coming back and remain competitive. Losing 3 cents a gallon on thousands of gallons of fuel seems like a failing model. However, he lived in the hope that if his gas was priced right the people would return to get their cars worked on or towed. He felt he could keep customers sticky with better prices, selling them snacks and items from the station when they came in. Customer retention means they will return to the station for more than just that one need. Some called it crazy, but he maintained this model throughout his nearly 40 years in the business—and it worked to a T. Through the years, other businesses have employed these sorts of tactics, but at the time in the early 80's it was ground-breaking. For example, now, on the shelves of a big box store like a Target or Wal-Mart, you may see an item like an electric candle warmer being sold at cost or at a loss to the retailer. However, adjacent to that product are the wax fragrances that will sell at a major profit in perpetuity. My dad was ahead of his time in valuing, not mere profit, but customer retention. When greed might call us to price everything, with the highest margins in mind, wisdom allows us to price in a sustainable manner—benefiting the consumer and the company.

I have always found it interesting that my dad would never say that he found success, and in those early days I am sure he didn't feel successful. On paper, many would call him a bonafide success, but it didn't quite register with him. Internally he had a constant desire to increase his position. Dissatisfied with last year's growth, he set his sights on breaking records again the following year. As you'll read soon, I've inherited this same sort of insatiable hunger for "the next venture."

Even with his success in the gas business, he was always in search of another magic bullet that would lead him to an even better financial position. He sold phones for Nextel, got into the racing business, and added U-Hauls to the station's offerings—although they were not profitable and were a lot of work. He was constantly moving toward *potential*.

Growing up I loved being at the station. As early as age seven I remember heading to the Exxon to run the register and pump gas. And we can't forget the cigarettes—I was enamored with selling those cigarettes. I am sure it was illegal and would have caused big trouble if it were discovered that I was peddling Marlboros, nevertheless, it was part of my first gig. At $1 a pop ($1.10 after tax), I sold thousands of packs and even stole a few for myself. They were nasty and I struggled to choke down the smoke, but I thought it was a cool look. Plus, everyone that worked there smoked and I thought I would fit in. This principle was something that I actually picked up from my dad. I noticed he was always able to fit in with the crowd he was serving. I have seen him in the presence of dignitaries and paupers—relating to both, in an effort to drive them to a common goal.

I spent lots of time at the Exxon station—more than anyone else in our family. Like a sponge I soaked up the business, discovering the oddities and quirks. My favorite part was the customer interaction. I have always loved talking with people, learning their stories and what their struggles and achievements were. I would always try to commit their stories to memory so I could ask them the next time they came in. Early on I was being schooled in customer loyalty. The fact is, so many people forget this principle as their business grows: without the loyal customer, the business is bankrupt. Customer loyalty is not is not a bonus to the business—it is the very building block of the business.

There was a lady that came in for full service once or twice a week in her silver Honda Accord. This meant

I pumped her gas, cleaned her windows, and checked fluid levels. She looked exactly like Cruella de Vil, white hair with black stripes and ironically, she always had her pup in the car with her. I made a habit of stealing a dog treat from the cookie jar at our house before work to give to Cruella's dog. Of course, it didn't hurt that she tipped very well, which was the only way I could get paid at the time. It's amazing what your mind will remember when your success depends on it!

I love working and I always have. Leisure time can only be enjoyed and maximized when prefaced by a healthy work-life. There have been times in my adult life where I have been forced to search for work or accept a job that would strangle my creativity by keeping me behind a desk for 60 hours a week. I have intentionally remained grateful for those times, though I am all the more grateful for the gigs where I can be interacting with the Cruellas of the world, owning my own destiny.

The business journey for my family growing up was not always rainbows and unicorns at the glorious service station. In fact, the early '90s was a very dark time for my family. My dad and some business partners had opened a Nascar sanctioned short track—which was a seasonal event in Virginia. The problem was, with 12 races a year, if you have one too many rainouts, you've lost your investment. That's exactly what happened. To compound matters, the U.S. economy went into a recession with millions losing their jobs over the course of a couple years as we entered the 1990s.

My mother was responsible for distracting creditors that came to collect on debts and vehicles, which was a mortifying experience. In one particular instance, my brothers and I had to physically hide as a creditor was seeking repayment on debt from an auto loan. The well dressed man even took the opportunity to peer through the front window of our house to see if anyone was home. It caused great tension and stress which continued throughout much of my childhood. This is just one of the many risks you run when choosing to own your own business—especially one that is leveraged. As a result of the failure, my dad and his partners were forced into bankruptcy, which tainted his reputation locally. To make matters worse, every year that followed on the day of the season opener, the papers would write about the failure. In these secondary endeavors he never found the success that he had with the original Exxon station.

Finding a balance between risk and reward is a major factor in launching a new venture. My earliest memories are of watching my dad navigate that tight rope. My wife, Kelly and I have experienced great pain from taking risks and sacrificing everything in pursuit of a dream—a dream of owning something we could pass to our children to make an impact on generations to come.

It may seem like there were more hardships and failures than successes, but we are better for it from a personal and biblical perspective. The scriptures say, *"Consider it all joy, my brethren, when you encounter various tri-*

als, knowing that the testing of your faith produces endurance. And let endurance have its perfect result, so that you may be perfect and complete, lacking in nothing" (James 1:2-4).

As faith-filled Christians we know the tension involved in trusting God to deliver. In some cases, we were trusting Him to resolve messes that I caused myself and in other instances, we simply had to play with the hand we were dealt. Our hope was supported by the Word of God. We desperately wanted to move closer to Jesus and represent Him well in an unbelieving marketplace. We wanted to navigate the tension of our business lives and spiritual lives with excellence, cross-pollinating the two as much as possible. In those endeavors we saw hardship, but the hardship did not define us.

"But may the God of all grace, who called us to His eternal glory by Christ Jesus, after you have suffered a while, perfect, establish, strengthen, and settle you." (1 Peter 1:5)

We have seen this very verse play out in our own home many times. Somehow God sees us through and the results do pay off in the long run. "Suffering a little while," as Peter states, may be the price necessary for being perfected, established, strengthened and settled. The truth is, though, when it comes to sacrifice, most people are not willing to pay the high price of success.

Understanding there will be things that take a back seat to your business is essential to moving forward in the pursuit of your dream. I believe that the world is full of dreamers that give up because of fear, challenges, and a sacrifice that appears to be too big to make. Decide before you start that you are going to see this through no matter what challenges come your way. The decision to keep going is not made when you hit a roadblock. The decision to keep going should be made before you even get started.

Profitable Problem Solving

Without a genuine understanding of your *why,* you and your endeavor will be quite fragile along the way. What is your *why*? To answer that question, you can ask yourself, "What problem does my passion solve? What question is answered by my dream?" The truth is, great ideas start with *perceiving* and then *meeting* a need. Money itself is simply a reward for solving problems for someone.

Discovering this *why* will anchor you along the way. People without this motivating mission statement will fold when the revenue drops or quit when people are difficult. To overcome big obstacles you need an even bigger driving force. The truth is, people are often sold on the idea of simply making a lot of money. Our culture breeds a desire to earn as much cash as we can. We will easily buy into the latest and greatest idea only to find out it leaves us empty and feeling unsuccessful. As great as earning income can be, if it is our sole motivator, our lives, businesses, and relationships will never be oriented properly.

Walt Disney, one of my heroes, was famous for meeting challenges and asking the question, "Why is this impossible?" He pushed the envelope and as a result, his legacy continues to be critical in the success of The Walt Disney Company. He famously said, "If you can dream it, you can do it." He understood his reason for being and didn't allow anything to keep him from fleshing it out. He knew how to detour, how to pivot, and how to take big hits on the chin. You and I need this same grit in navigating failure. Ask yourself questions like, "How will I respond to trials?" and, "Who will I turn to when it seems impossible to succeed?" These questions will develop an attitude within that says, "I cannot fail. I have no other choice but to succeed."

Obstacles in your success won't always be numbers and figures, but are often people. Many will find fault in what you are doing and attempting. There will be many detractors from the course you are on. It is imperative that you maintain your *why* and keep track with your God-given dream. I have seen this play out in my own pursuits when, at times, my own friends and relatives called me crazy and some abandoned me in my pursuit altogether. I have even been left to stand alone with no support on a few occasions. Digging your heels into your *why* and continuing to meet your perceived need in the marketplace will remedy the temporary blowbacks.

Money is not necessarily some great accomplishment, it is merely the result of a good question that's met with a great answer. I can assure you that when you begin to branch out there will be times of lean operations before financial success. Ask yourself, "Am I willing to endure stress and insecurity *now* to reap success *later?*" Most people would answer yes, but it is easier said than done. It is especially difficult in the fourth quarter, 4th and 10, with no time outs and you're far from the goal line.

I am not someone who gives up easily. I will hang on until the last strand of the thread finally breaks. The truth is, sheer grit and passion are not enough to find success in business. Rather, innovatively answering questions before they are asked is crucial in developing an accomplished business. If you don't begin with the hard questions, you will lack answers and ultimately, lack your *why.*

Are you willing to make sacrifices to, for example, have the cash to pay employees for 6-8 months while your business finds its footing? Are you able to pay all debt associated with your business and personal life without financial profit for 1-2 years before you see the operation move into the black? Are you and your spouse both equally married to the business? Most companies fail before they even have a chance. I have consulted on hundreds of ideas that were dead on arrival due to a *lack of planning.*

I often relate marriage to business in that many couples plan more for their wedding day than their young married life, which is far more critical to the success of the marriage. Our culture is obsessed with the imagery, planning and idea of a wedding, but struggles to confront what 60 years of devotion looks like and how to properly plan ahead. As business owners, we often salivate over the idea of a *launch* and we make big arrangements for grand openings. Ribbon cuttings are great, but they aren't enough and will never magically sustain revenue. It takes more, it takes a *why.*

Whether you grew up in an environment or entrepreneurship, or you missed that train altogether, problem solving and *why* discovery is critical for eventual success. Here's the thing, no one can discover that *for* you. It requires a personal pursuit on your part. Simon Sinek once wrote, "The combination of your WHY and HOW is as exclusively yours as your fingerprint." Whether your next pursuit is a startup business, homeschooling children, taking on a promotion, or joining a local club—the *why* behind your efforts is completely unique and completely necessary for your long-term success. Find it now so you aren't lost later.

CHAPTER TWO

GETTING PERSONAL

"**I**T'S NOT PERSONAL, it's business," is a phrase often coined in Hollywood and echoed throughout culture. The truth is, our personal lives and business lives are often intertwined. For instance, a messy marriage can wreck a business. Inversely, a poorly executed investment can harm one's family. The overlap of personal lives and business lives has often been ignored or rejected altogether. Some of my foundational personal experiences not only impacted my personal life, for better or worse, but my business life too.

Much of my childhood was composed of intense and undeserved scrutiny. I suffered both physical and mental abuse at the hands of many throughout my early years and it even lingered into my college days. I often felt a sense of responsibility for the abuse because it seemed to follow me throughout many seasons and areas of life, despite my efforts to overcome it. Somehow I felt guilty, as if I were attracting the abuse.

In my early teens, I would lay by the door early in the morning to not miss my dad's drive into the station for work. I desperately wanted to be included, to belong. Frequently, though, my dad and older brother would leave our house through another door so that I would not be alerted to them exiting together. I tried to hang on for as long as I could, but it became obvious that neither my brother nor my dad wanted me to be involved in operating the business. The reason for my lack of inclusion remains a mystery. It may have been my age or perhaps my personality. Growing up I was generally the louder one of my two siblings. An extrovert to the core, I was a tad out of place among my more quiet and introspective brothers.

There came a time when my dad and my older brother grew in their relationship. They became great friends, business partners, and confidantes. He, by far, did not have the passion I had for the Exxon station, but he was more skilled with automobile repairs and seemed to be better suited for taking over the business...and that is exactly what happened. Over time, the transfer of power, ownership, and leadership came to fruition and eventually my brother was gifted with the sole ownership of this very successful business. Unfortunately there was no discussion about my potential role or equity position at all. It was sort of like being cut out of a will, before the benefactor passes.

At home, my father was emotionally abusive, frequently expressing his dissatisfaction with my choices and performance. I would constantly adjust who I was to fit his idea of who I should be, though it was never enough. Much of his disdain for me was rooted in a lack of interest in the things that interested me. For example, I am a creative person who also loves organization and methods, an unusual combination for my father to understand. I live in the marriage of artistry and administration. I enjoy music while he drives in silence. I appreciate artistic expression while he has little use for it. The arts and conscientiousness are not ventures that easily produce income, so he never understood my affinity toward them.

My fifth grade year I tried out for the Gilbert Linkous Elementary (GLE) Sharps, our school choir. I was a nervous wreck and was never able to talk with anyone in my family about it. I thank God for my choir teacher, Ms. Podsednick (Ms. P), who recognized some musical talent within me and encouraged me to pursue the choir. There were two groups: one would be the 'A' choir, that would perform and compete while representing the school. The other was the lesser 'B' choir with fewer commitments throughout the year. Ms. P thought I had what it would take to make the Sharps A choir. I found the courage within me to go for it. After trying out I was delighted to learn that I made the group!

Thrilled beyond measure, I felt like I had won the lottery. That excitement was doused fairly quickly when I realized I had no one at home to tell. Daily I left home with a promise that my mother would pick me up from school later that afternoon yet everyday she did not show. I am not sure I blame her, as she was under the same torture I was in the home. She too experienced constant, insufferable abuse from my father. I know that she had a hard time keeping it together, which left her mind scattered. She attempted to shield me, but it was a futile task to do so. I would wait for hours at school for someone to pick me up and I don't recall a single time that anyone came. I learned to walk a few miles to the Exxon station and even walked the long way home on a few occasions.

Getting selected for the Sharps meant that we would practice after school and I knew it would mean that I would have to walk everyday. But, I did it because it was a creative outlet for me—an escape even. When Christmas came we had tryouts for solos and I was honored with the lead in the German folk tune "Still, still, still."

I distinctly remember every lyric and every note to this day. Ms. P worked tirelessly with me—likely sensing that I wasn't receiving any support at home. We worked together for months and finally the night came for my performance. The audience was dark and the stage lights were bright and I made it through, thanks to Ms. P. It was my first taste of public performance and I somehow knew it would not be my last. I have to admit that

I don't remember any of my family being there. In fact, I think a neighbor brought me to the school that night. While this neglect was devastating and haunts me still, I promised myself that I would never allow that abuse to define my future or my potential for success. Regrettably, and I believe as a result of being in an atmosphere of neglect, I also suffered sexual abuse from multiple boys and men when I was young. My earliest recollection of sexual abuse was at the age of seven. My older brother had disgusting friends who would play on my emotions and coerce me into doing things that I still see when I close my eyes. Beyond that, men connected to the Exxon station would capture me and take me to their home and abuse me. I was frequently left with no reasonable escape. I would walk from their homes the same way I would walk home from GLE—with no one to tell. Soon I had convinced myself that the problem was me. I figured, *Why else would this consistent abuse occur?*

The depth of my pain, regret, and shame still haunt me today, though I've found measures of healing. I have always felt a sense of responsibility for the actions of these abusers which is not uncommon for a victim. The conflict in me was always that somehow if I was responsive to those that were taking advantage of me I would somehow gain their favor, just as I craved my father's approval. Deep pain and immense rejection for my entire childhood had led me to seek their approval. It would never come because they weren't actually interested in me, they were more interested in satisfying their own grotesque desires. I was simply a pawn in their scheme to find their sexual and emotional needs met. Yet, I found myself longing for their approval no less.

I spent years—decades even—reliving those moments over and over again and the details never left my mind. In a moment, I can return to the musty smell of wood and wet dog from the old house where the abuser would take me. He had two roommates, one male with blond hair and one female with dyed red and blond hair. They had to know what was going on, yet laughed and joked like it was nothing. I remember the smell of beer on their breath as we played card games and the smell of the charcoal grill simmering on the porch. I had never seen a grill that used charcoal, we used a gas one at home. The smell of the laundry detergent from the sheets of his bed, the taste of Hamburger Helper Beef Stroganoff, his crooked teeth too close for comfort. All of the subtle and not-so-subtle sights and smells were branded in my young mind.

Often I will come across these same smells and tastes and it brings me right back to the most painful moments of my life. I distinctly remember lying in bed next to a grown man who was begging for my attention and essentially forcing me to touch his sweat-drenched body. It was disgusting. I felt guilty, he had falsely felt like a friend to me, lured me with funny games and television shows that interested a kid. How could I feel bad for such a repugnant person? I got out of that house as quick as

I could and have never mentioned these moments until the writing of this book.

The thought of these actions have affected every area of my life: my marriage, my relationship with my parents, how I live and interact with my kids, and even my personal drive to become successful in life and business. As awful as these moments might be to recall, I find that in a way they motivate me.

My testimony is a love story—specifically my learning of and accepting God's love. In many ways I could not comprehend a love like His, unconditional love from a Father. The love of my earthly father has always been based on conditions, based on what I could achieve or prove to him. In my constant pursuit of his approval, I learned as a child that I would never achieve or attain his love. My understanding of God was always tainted by my perception of a father, one that was never home, always seeking, and taking more in order to achieve success. I viewed God just like my earthly father, a father who would allow me to be forced into that musty house to be taken advantage of. It took years to clear up my perceptions of God and find myself rooted in who He truly is.

A very personal and beautiful passage of scripture that helped me along is found in Isaiah 43. It's a gorgeous description of how God speaks to and thinks of His children:

"But now, this is what the Lord says— he who

created you, Jacob, he who formed you, Israel: 'Do not fear, for I have redeemed you; I have summoned you by name; you are mine. When you pass through the waters, I will be with you; and when you pass through the rivers, they will not sweep over you. When you walk through the fire, you will not be burned; the flames will not set you ablaze. For I am the Lord your God, the Holy One of Israel, your Savior; I give Egypt for your ransom, Cush and Seba in your stead. Since you are precious and honored in my sight, and because I love you, I will give people in exchange for you, nations in exchange for your life." (Isaiah 43:1-4)

Grasping the idea that I was the beloved of God was challenging for me, but became a lifelong pursuit that I began early on. I came to understand this love at age 10 during a church camp. At this particular camp, a clear presentation of Christ was given. Moved with newfound conviction and love, I accepted the Lord, but with very little to fan the flame at home the former life recaptured me and little changed. God, in His fiery love, continued to pursue our family. My mother had always been more of the spiritual leader in the home. Sweet, unassuming, and kind—she prayed for us fervently and grew in her connection with Jesus. She was the polar opposite of my dad.

During my early teens we belonged to the Church of Christ—attending weekly services and volunteering along the way. While at a wedding at age 15, our household direction changed. At the reception my dad met a Church of God pastor and they really meshed well. My dad was an unfeeling man, a bit of a stoic, who was not generally inclined toward spirituality. Yet, for some reason this particular pastor made an impression on him. Following that event my dad said, "If we start going to the Church of God where that man pastors, I'll go to church too."

Thus, our family began attending that church. My mom and I rededicated ourselves afresh to Jesus. I began to understand God's love and grace for me in a more real way. My youth pastor was great, she loved me and challenged me to know God more deeply. She taught me that God's plan wasn't about me, but about Him. It was as if God had washed me clean and no matter what fire I faced or what giant came my way—I knew I was His beloved.

I wish I could tell you that my earthly father is a different man today, but he is not. What I can say is that *I am a different man*. Everyday is a challenge, but when I wake up and when I lie down, I can say with full assurance that, "I am His beloved." Through that work in me, God has allowed some reconciliation between my father and I. I can finally see him through God's eyes as His beloved as well.

Early into this newfound life, I got involved in a youth group, volunteering, and attending events. During those years I met a girl named Kelly who attended a different church, but under the same denomination. I recall a youth convention at Virginia Beach where we volunteered together and became close friends.

Being geographically separated, at different churches, and without the internet to assist our communication, our friendship was somewhat on hold. In the meantime I took my first job at a church day care and in the summers I worked for some church members in a nearby neighborhood who had two kids. I planned activities and kept them busy in the summer. While taking the kids to a local pool, I was delighted to learn my old friend Kelly was working there as a lifeguard. We picked up where we left off. By then she had other dating interests and began talking about some guy she was potentially going to marry. Somewhere in my heart, whether consciously or unconsciously, I knew she was the one. Boldly I said to her, "You aren't going to marry that guy," which caught her off guard, but I wasn't wrong. To no one's surprise, my trips to the pool were more frequent for the duration of that summer.

A New Season

After high school I moved on to college in Florida which was one of the best choices I have ever made. Getting out of Virginia was an escape, even with continued abuse from home by telephone and email. I had received some verbal attacks while in college, mostly rooted in misunderstandings, but I was much safer there. I excelled in that environment, considering my childhood home wasn't weighing me down. I began to study music with the goal of becoming a music minister down the road.

To my surprise, I was not the only one in our family enrolling in college during that time. My dad had a computer science degree from Virginia Tech. When he learned I would be studying ministry in Florida, he enrolled in similar coursework and eventually earned a doctorate from Asbury Theological Seminary. Many found it strange and some speculated that he did so simply to prevent me from acquiring credentials and knowledge that he himself didn't have. The jury is still out.

Nevertheless, by 2004 when I was wrapping up college, he decided that he had spent too much on my education. During school he had co-signed with me to buy a home in Florida, which I proceeded to renovate and care for. After I had sold the home for a profit, he informed me that I would be paying for my last two semesters in college out of pocket, meanwhile he paid for his own. I point this out because somehow, it felt as though my own father was in competition with me. Did he perceive me as a threat? Was he nervous about setting me up for success? The questions still loom.

By that time, my old friend Kelly was no longer a friend, but a fiance. After graduating with honors, I used the funds from my home-sale to pay for our wedding. It felt as though I had received a reset button for life. She was and is such an incredible blessing. She was the perfect balance to my fast-paced pursuits. While she has not always understood this pursuit of success, she has always supported it, even when the idea was a dumb one.

On one occasion she told me that it didn't matter where we were or what we were doing—because as long as she was with me, she was happy. Those words have a way of sticking in a man's heart. She has been pushed to the absolute limits of her capacity, stretched to develop new skills and has persevered with grace and dignity. She has also had some really incredible ideas along the way. My partnership with her has been the very best decision I have ever made in business and in life. I never would have made it this far without her.

Missing Nostalgia

Whenever I was back in Virginia for a visit, I would always drive through town to see the Exxon, to take in the nostalgia and relive some fond childhood memories. On one particular trip home on a break from college, I recall visiting the station and pulling into a place that was unrecognizable, frankly. It was being renovated at the time. My mother and father had built a new home and moved in during that year of college. My dad had almost stepped out of the shop entirely by that point and it was my brother's show now. He had devised a plan to relocate the shop to a beautiful building a few blocks from the original and rename it. This was all news to me. I had never dreamt of something that I truly loved becoming a place so foreign to me. My dad was seeking to retire completely and my brother would take over full operation of the Exxon. My brother had big dreams and I will hand it to him, he knows how to dream big. Together, they negotiated a lease for the real estate at the current Exxon location and my brother moved the business up the street to that brand new, state of the art facility. The shift in facility was not the only change for them. They sold out to a brand new business model that was focused on maximizing repair orders, studying shop performance, and becoming the 'go-to' shop in our community, which has done very well. It is a beautiful shop— so clean you could eat off the floor. The truth is, I could feel like I missed out on the opportunity, but perhaps in God's economy I only missed out on a headache. If no door was going to be open there, I would have to go elsewhere and build one. I still had a passion to pursue my own business, but I had to do it on my own. This desire has led me wrong in many instances, including many of which I am not very proud of. Nevertheless, the successes have tipped the scale in my favor.

The proverbial saying rings true: life is not fair. In fact, it's not about being fair, it's about your response to the wrong that positions you for success. I began to realize that it's not about what has been handed to you in life, it's what you do with the deck you have been dealt. In realizing this, I grew by leaps and bounds during that season in Florida. I was responsible for my own workload in school, my household, and worked 2-3 jobs to somehow prove that I could pull it off.

I am not sure how I was able to maintain my work

ethic during these years, but I seemed to find a strange peace running on all cylinders. It was a place of comfort for me. I have always worked at a quick pace in an effort to constantly prove my value to an organization which has afforded me some incredible opportunities throughout my career.

I have always loved *business work* more than I have loved *church work*. I studied ministry in college and thought that this would be enough to pursue and almost protect myself from the risk of being an entrepreneur. I had seen my father's failures in business and wanted to insulate myself from those pitfalls by studying ministry and avoiding business altogether. I couldn't have been more wrong.

Once I had graduated and married Kelly we had to sort out what our next steps in life would look like. We had a season where I worked retail jobs. I worked in Hobby Lobby, learning the culture and the corporate structure. Eventually I managed a team and was on track to grow into higher levels of management. Meanwhile, Kelly worked at a makeup counter in a store at the mall, eventually overseeing the department. Shortly after that, she was offered a position as district manager. Until then, our early marriage had been spent in lean times financially. With me slated to climb into middle management and her moving into district management, we foresaw big career advancement and a much healthier paycheck. Not only that, but this would be a phenomenal resume credential and experience moving ahead.

Not everyone is an entrepreneur. Some are intrapreneurs. For instance, Steve Ballmer is worth nearly 80 billion dollars at the time of this writing. You would think he acquired his wealth by starting and selling a company or companies. In reality, he worked within Microsoft as an employee for decades, navigating the ranks cleverly and taking advantage of stock options and new opportunities. He didn't found or own Microsoft, yet he worked his way up as an employee and achieved remarkable financial success.

You may have a burning passion for business without a deep desire to actually start one. In these cases, you may be called to intrapreneurship. Perhaps you lock arms with a company and ride out their growth, working your way up along the way and perhaps eventually taking an equity position in the business. There are countless success stories of regular employees who brought their entrepreneurial spirit into a business and climbed the ranks as a result.

For us, we were on track to do just that sort of thing in our respective careers. However, after much pursuit by our respective companies, we reluctantly declined because I accepted a position at a church in Missouri. The truth is, we still wrestle with the rightness or wrongness of that decision, unsure of our final conclusion on this matter. On one hand, management could have given us a remarkable skill set and stepping stones for our calling. On the other, we did feel in our hearts like ministry was an irrevocable part of our calling.

We packed our bags and moved to Missouri where I was the Worship Pastor, and Kelly was Children's Church Pastor. I have often looked back on this moment and regretted this decision because choosing to pursue the above mentioned management positions would have been a lot better for us in the long term. Making the right moves would have made me a little more employable later in life, when I needed the credit. Nevertheless, we have learned that the regrets of the past do nothing for your future self.

While serving at the church in Missouri, I purchased my first house to flip, in order to supplement my ministry income. My entrepreneurial engine had no off switch. With my home in Florida I had gained ample experience in renovation and handyman projects. I was familiar with the overall process and inputs. We restored the kitchen, bathrooms, flooring, paint, and we did quality work. I remember when I showed my family the first house flip. Kelly and I had returned home for the holidays and I had made a video of the pictures from before and after. My dad was complimentary, but could not figure out how I could have accomplished it on my own. The flip looked great and every detail was touched by me personally. It was as if he didn't think that I could have been as handy as I was.

The truth is, I couldn't allow his perception of me to put a ceiling in my life. Never let someone else's opinion of you determine your limitations. The lesson to be learned from these seasons is that most people do not have multi-million dollar businesses or ideas handed to them. Most successes have been self-taught, self-lived, self-pursued, and take much time and effort to develop. Almost always the journey to success is marred with many failures. Most people have seasons when they give time, their personal lives, and money before they achieve the success that becomes their livelihood.

Our ministry time in Missouri was good, but not permanent. After feeling that our tenure there was up, we resigned and moved back to Virginia. Our tails were tucked, as we felt we had failed. The conditions of the market following the house renovation were awful. As a result we held the property for too long, went through several renters, and ultimately could not sell the property. Being geographically separated from the house exacerbated the challenges. Eventually the house was foreclosed by the bank. Our time in the Show Me State felt like a failure.

To recoup I pursued multiple harebrained ideas like photography, wedding planning, and 'No Down Payment' real estate deals, all of which were unsuccessful, and often came at a great expense to our family. These times were always hard and made me question my abilities. I always knew that I had the capacity for success, but I wasn't quite settled on how I was going to get there.

My early career was experiencing failure after failure and ultimately affected my drive to continue. But I resolved that I would become successful someday and prove wrong those who were against me.

It was this relentless pursuit that drained our family financially dry in the early years. Our situation was unstable and the income had been consistently low. As a result, Kelly and I found ourselves in a deep hole financially. We had not been irresponsible with our money in terms of loads of personal debt or pursuing dangerous ventures—we simply weren't making enough to make ends meet. We were saddled in business debt, struggling to save money, and desiring more for our family.

By then Kelly and I had two beautiful girls. Fatherhood changed me, as it changes most men, in more ways than can be counted. I felt the weight of responsibility and the joy of it also. I knew I needed to be more calculated and measured. I was steadfast in my desire to give them a different upbringing than what I had.

I remember being very restless one night and finally deciding to just get out of bed. My thoughts swirled and anxiety set in. I felt stuck, tied to debts and with very little in the way of hope. I thought a lot, prayed a lot, and went into my girls room hoping to find some encouragement. As I watched them sleep peacefully I knew I had to do something. When the sun began to rise the next morning, Kelly and I talked and made the excruciating decision to file personal bankruptcy, to try to find our footing and start fresh.

I was humiliated. I thought it was important to let our employer know and I did. I have always felt like they never saw me the same after breaking the news to them. It was the lowest I have ever been in my life. How could someone with my skill set let his family down by this much? I know that there are others that have faced this same predicament with the same outcome, which is to question everything we know about ourselves. It was during this time that we had to seek a safety net for our children and sought government assistance to ensure our kids had what they needed. I believe in these government programs as intended; a short term safety net to help families get on the right foot and move forward to find success. I remember the phone call like it was yesterday. I called our local assistance office and quickly found out that we definitely qualified for food assistance; food stamps.

As part of the sign up process our kids had to have a health checkup at the local Social Security office. I remember crying in the bathroom of the doctor's office as I heard our daughter's crying pleas from finger pricks to ensure her vitamin levels were in a safe zone. I decided at that moment I would never let my dreams die. My family was depending on me to make something out of nothing.

Ideation

People will struggle to understand you. They will encourage you (sometimes wrongfully) to seek a more stable and consistent income. I have listened to those voices myself, especially after my children were born. When I looked into the beautiful eyes of my children, I saw a deep sense of responsibility that I had never felt before. It inspired a longing for success *for them,* and not as much for me. I couldn't live as risky as before, chasing every idea like it was an be-all and end-all solution.

The problem was I still had ideas swirling around in my head. I have a condition where I can look at something, analyze it quickly, and identify potential opportunities within minutes of being introduced to it. I have used this strategy in many business and nonprofit settings while coaching throughout my career.

The truth is, I cannot physically or emotionally act on every idea that runs through my thoughts. As a result, I have developed over time a simple little formula to run my ideas through before sharing them openly. If I were honest I have at least 2-3 ideas daily that I could legitimately execute and might have a positive return, but I would be run ragged in the pursuit. I like to run these ideas through a filter that intentionally scrutinizes them so as not to overwhelm myself. In turn, I am leaving *good things* behind in an effort to pursue the *greater things* for me and my contribution to the world.

The filter questions go something like this: Does this idea solve an inverse need? Does it have mass appeal? Have I encountered this perceived need more than 5 times in the last 2 weeks? If the idea passes these tests and I can find full and complete justification, I run it through a second, even more scrutinous filter, my wife Kelly. She has incredible perception and a practicality that makes a good balance for me. She has honestly assessed and provided invaluable advice over the years and runs a nearly perfect track record of analysis and wise counsel. Find someone in your life that is not afraid to be honest with you while being sensitive to your entrepreneurial spirit. The entrepreneurial spirit, like mine, is creative, but also very sensitive. I know that not all my ideas are great. But when I really hit one that passes all of the tests it usually finds success. After pouring out my passion and thoughts into an idea, I end up identifying with it. So, when an idea is scrutinized it feels like I am being personally rejected. This has been one of the biggest lessons for me throughout my career. You are not your ideas. An idea might be shut down—but that does not mean that *you* are.

Once Kelly, my counsel, reviews the idea, she will give me constructive feedback that I need to make adjustments and then re-present it with a more solid foundation. Keep in mind, at this point in ideation it is all still internal and we haven't shared this outside of the safety of our relationship.

Identifying, knowing, and trusting your internal team is a key to the success of any entrepreneur. You need people in your life and business who will honestly assess your ideas and give you constructive feedback. Whether this is a spouse, a pastor, a business mentor, a coach, or a combination—you need a team around you who will listen to your pitches and delicately shoot holes in them. It is imperative that you not surround yourself with 'yes' people, but rather people who support you in true honesty.

Unknowingly, this process has proven positive for me as I have been in many situations where I had to sell my idea. This early scrutiny has forced me to fully think through, and reveal every flaw, prior to presenting (or selling) to high level decision makers. There is no substitute for being fully prepared to share your big idea.

During this season of life, as we picked up pieces and began again, new ideas were rising to the surface. One idea in particular, was passing every litmus test I had. I felt I had harnessed a concept that could not only be profitable, but could shake up an industry.

CHAPTER THREE

SOMETHING NEW, AGAIN

"See, I am doing a new thing! Now it springs up; do you not perceive it? I am making a way in the wilderness and streams in the wasteland." (Isaiah 43:19)

KELLY AND I had been stewing on an idea for several years. We wanted to build something not yet seen in the marketplace. If one thing was certain, it was that American restaurant culture was always changing. Fast food emerged in the 50s and 60s. This was naturally followed by a drive-thru window craze in the 70s. The 80s and saw an uptick in casual dining with salad bars and buffets rising to prominence. The 90s were marked by a rise in pizza delivery and diverse options on menus.

By the 2000s, particularly 2007-2008, restaurant trends were moving to a fast casual experience.

Restaurateurs were tearing down walls, creating open seating, showing off their kitchens, and giving the consumers more personalization options. Many of the heavy hitters in fast food were struggling to find their footing in an uncertain market and economy. The millennial generation were, and are, the most coveted shoppers, and biggest spenders from retail to foods, and adapting to that market proved to be challenging for the burger joints of yesteryear. We began by asking some questions.

Could we provide a fresh alternative to the dessert market that would appeal to the ever growing Millennial shopper segment? Could we locally source ingredients to have a meaningful impact in our community? What if all of the items could be made in-house and fresh daily? Could we create an experience catering to families? Could we create flavors and tastes unlike anything else available?

We began with the *need* and then made our plans to disrupt the dessert industry that had historically relied on brand recognition and grocery presence to drive the train. Until now. We gave birth to our idea–Crumb & Get It Cookie Company. The concept, while simple, would take some education for our customers because it wasn't being done anywhere else. We would welcome guests into the shop, present them with a variety of doughs and mix-ins, then bake the cookies hot and fresh for them while they waited. The process beginning to end would take about 10 minutes, but the end result would be custom, made-to-order cookies.

The perceived need was presented, the idea was constructed, and we passed it through various levels of scrutiny. My wheels were turning 100 miles per hour as I finally landed on something that I knew would be a hit. There were so many things that I had observed in the market that were taking off, especially with my targeted demographic. A few years earlier, this would have been a suicidal move for a business, but things had changed. Restaurateurs were opening up dining rooms and bringing in more light to help deflect from the previously popular darker dining environments. Nearly every business leader, food or not, was working to tell a story rather than mill out sales or distinguish themselves as the cheapest, fastest option. The race to zero was no longer viable. Retailers were scrambling to find ways to amend their business model from discount shopping and sales to create a narrative that would appeal to the current demands of the market. Nowadays, storytelling is almost synonymous with marketing. At the time, this was avant garde.

Shoppers were willing to spend more if they knew the company was committed to a cause. We were making an impact on our community from day one because we began with the need. It is imperative that any approach be nimble. Ideas, trends, audiences, and preferences change especially quickly in the instant, digital world we live in. Change is inevitable and must be embraced throughout life. This is the essence of Isaiah 43:19, the verse that began this chapter. God defines and reveals, moment by moment in our lives. He is concerned with every finite detail of who we are. Our development is important to Him. Most importantly in life and in business we must make the choice to embrace His leadership in all. Believe me, I have tried it both ways. Pursuing Him, or pursuing a reliance on my abilities. The former works much better. Let Him do a new thing, in you and in your business. When you make a commitment to follow Jesus, you are making a commitment to pivot, change plans, uproot, and adapt on a continual basis.

Much like the current changes in the marketplace, our concept store would be spatially open. Our Cookie Designers, as we would call our employees, would walk with the guests through the process, and ultimately create a unique experience in our shop. The smells would be scrumptious and well thought out, the taste would be 'not too sweet' as the current consumer demanded. The atmosphere would be fun and driven by recycled materials to make our footprint sustainable. Our cookies would be hot and fresh, rather than sitting in a case or package for purchase. The guest experience in our shop would be unsurpassed.

The atmosphere in the shop was fun. We often received compliments as we provided an opportunity for families, couples, and friends to come together and converse while they waited on their cookies to bake. We had incorporated Table Talk cards that encouraged conversation by providing questions to open up discussions to pass the time; a detail that was well received.

Not everyone will immediately understand something new, but if they *never* understand it—that's on me. This new model for a cookie shop, and many more ideas, ran around in my head and I decided to meet with our first architect to put feet on some of these ideas. She completely missed the concept. We left with a menagerie of ideas that would ultimately be produced in our first shop...but these ideas missed the atmosphere we were going for.

We had wrongly relied upon the architect to guide our color choices and atmosphere which led to a terrible end result. Yellow-gold walls, teal and blue accents, and a hint of fake brick ruined our in-shop experience for the highly perceptive consumers. One of our favorite ideas was to have a portion of the store isolated from the general public for special events. We ended up with a set of round tables in the middle of the shop and no hope of partitioned guests. This was another costly mistake for us. While having a trusted team to scrutinize ideas is critical, you also need a trusted team to facilitate and execute on those ideas. Frankly, I had wrongly delegated our interior design.

I remember feeling totally disappointed in the end product visually, especially the space we had created as we followed the plan of the architect. This was an example of my failure to thoroughly communicate a new idea and concept to my support team. I blame myself for this failure.

The location of our first store was good and bad. It was good in that the proximity to Virginia Tech campus was incredible. It was bad because of the building itself. The store had no solid parking solution. We were dependent on street parking availability. If there were no spots, folks had to park in a paid garage that was behind us. As a result, we were relying heavily on foot traffic and local shoppers to stop in.

We had a number of delays that would derail construction, but we learned many things during this process. I kept my focus on always learning what could be done better. I said from day one that this idea was meant for duplication. The first store would come with battle scars, but the subsequent locations would be more well conceived.

I worked hard marketing in the months leading up to opening. We wanted to build as much anticipation as possible. I had reached out to our local newspaper and the college paper as well. I had met with countless businesses and leaders. We had signage facing the college campus and on Main Street.

We were hometown people, graduated from the hometown high school, we had many friends and family there to support us. In general we felt good about our product. Six months had passed from greenlighting the concept to cutting the ribbon at our first location. We had personally funded the business ourselves and were ready to see, not only a return, but a solid community impact. Despite the predictable ups and downs, we worked within what we were given and opened with much fanfare.

We opened on a game weekend in the college town of Virginia Tech in Blacksburg, Virginia. The shop was less than a mile from the football stadium and we never could have imagined the crowd that would come in. The shop was absolutely packed, shoulder to shoulder inside, with a line leading outside. Our goodies were flying off the shelf.

One of my favorite stories occurred on opening day for our Blacksburg shop. We were cranking out cookies, throwing flour and sugar around, and a middle aged gentleman came up to the counter and motioned for me to join him for a chat. I remember having the thought, *I don't have time for this, what is this guy thinking?* I went over and he said his son was "sick" outside, meaning he had thrown up. He assured me that they had not entered the shop and our goodies were not to blame.

I felt sorry for the family and I grabbed a bucket and cleaning supplies and headed out the door to meet this young child and his family. When I arrived on scene I quickly discovered that there was no *sick young child.* Instead, it was his 20-year-old son who had been drinking since 8 a.m. and had thrown up on our patio outside. He could barely stand. I expected a pitiable child and instead got a drunk college student. I looked over at the family and all I could think to say was, "I think it would be best if you guys left." I cleaned up the mess and headed back into the shop for more madness.

It was quite the welcome to the cookie business.

Adaptation

We maintained those crowds for the remainder of the fall and over time local newspapers would publish something that would cause another influx of customers. We maintained that pace until January 1. Until that moment, I had no idea that a sweets business dies in January every year. New diet plans, resolutions, and bad weather create a perfect storm for slow business. It was another opportunity for us to adapt and amend our model to find our footing. I saw this slumping trend in every shop, every year from then on. We went from moving at an incredible pace, to a near standstill within a week's time.

I was thrilled with how things had gone up to this point, but now we were sitting around doing nothing everyday. Eventually, I got the idea to walk across the street and check in on our friend, and manager of the largest book seller for Virginia Tech at the time, Mike. We had developed a relationship during construction and I was at a loss. I noticed while visiting with Mike that students were returning their books for the semester and in return the bookstore was giving out free burger coupons from a Burger King across town. I asked Mike if he would consider making Crumb & Get It his official partner and we would provide coupons for the students. At that moment I had an epiphany that I would sell coupons to Mike at a discounted rate that would allow us to quickly ramp up our volume during the downturn. We would then offer a free cookie to each guest that had returned books and received the coupon in the bookstore. Also, it worked out to be significantly cheaper for the bookstore, making it a win-win. I've learned that negotiations are not win-lose scenarios. A good negotiation does not result in one party holding the short end of the stick. Instead, a sound negotiation allows all parties to win with a mutual "thank you" at the end.

One Saturday, before the end of the semester, Mike came in and said, "Are you sure you guys can handle this?" I remember thinking that I wasn't 100% sure, but I needed his business so I enthusiastically said, "Yes, we got this!" I've learned to always give the *perception* that you can handle it, even if you are unsure. For better or worse, *ready, fire, aim*, is standard operating procedure for entrepreneurs.

While I may have been a little unsure of the processes, the storage, and the Cookie Designers, I never doubted my ability to figure it out, even if it was hard. I have shared this story often in consulting settings, speaking about the ability for every business to adapt in a challenging situation. I have always been honest in my assessment of my personal ability to perform as required for the task. Sometimes in interviews, when asked what I would do in a setting where I was unsure of exactly how to accomplish something, I chimed in with, "Give me 24 hours, and I'll have your answer." Of course, this leans on my ability to seek and find solutions to the most challenging of circumstances. I always bathe these times with prayer, seeking the full will of God in any and all opportunities.

Mike and I made it happen and during the next semester we distributed thousands of cookies in return for those coupons. This simple plan would sustain us in and out of season from then on. It introduced our unique store to nearly every new student coming to Virginia Tech. And it helped us maintain a top-of-mind presence with nearly every student there. Additionally, we created a great bond with Mike as we delivered on every promise we made to him. The result was a near doubling of foot traffic during those down months.

We worked the bookstore concept throughout the rest of our time developing Crumb & Get It. We developed relationships with businesses and community leaders and worked together to grow our presence in the market.

Working with the University bookstore allowed me to cross-pollinate ideas. I figured if we could step out of our store to sell coupons to the university, we could step out of our store for other ventures as well. This idea launched an entirely new arm of our business called catering. Suddenly, we could deliver your wedding cookies to your venue. We could create gifts for your business clients for the holidays. We could cater your child's birthday party with handmade goodies. We would often do this for customers, always promising to never spill the beans if they wanted to tell partygoers that they hand-made the goodies. This spoke to the high quality and care we took in hand-making our products. This was a key step to help us through the winter months and avoid much leaner times. While foot traffic in March might be lean, folks are still having birthday parties and weddings, and we capitalized on this.

Many people start something new and think that business will come to them. They will say, "The concept is good enough," or "My product is the best," without any plan to bring people in. I've seen some really good ideas go up in flames because a developer was unwilling to pay the price of time and effort to find new customers. It is an arrogant place to dwell when you assume that the customers will somehow find you. Henry Ford once said that you, "Cannot afford to *not* advertise."

In an ever evolving digital and direct-to-consumer marketplace we must learn how important our pursuit is. Some prior fan base will result in a tribe of evangels if your product is good, but nothing can benefit you more than a consistent flow of new customers every day.

Some of this pursuit was successful and some was not so successful, but I never let it stop me from pursuing my customers. Most businesses fail because of an unworkable model. Yet many businesses fail, even with a workable model, because they fail when it comes to customer acquisition. If customer acquisition costs are high, you can get customers in the store, but they may not profit you enough to recoup your marketing budget.

These things have to be balanced out with laser-like precision.

This sort of thoughtful marketing is essential. I am not talking about traditional forms of marketing, like print ads and billboards. In fact the nontraditional forms are far more effective in today's market. But these strategies can also ruin a business's image. How many businesses flood your social media with the same post 2700 times a day? They're often mimicking the perceived success of someone else. How many others copy and paste successful businesses applying the same strategy, unsuccessfully, to their own? Truth is, easy marketing has never been successful for any business. Even large corporations fall into this trap, never innovating, and as a result, lack in any success.

If you're not leading, you're following. If businesses are copying what you're doing, then you are doing something right. Ineffective marketing is a pet peeve of mine. Many ideas make excellent businesses, but have the wrong message. Effective messaging changes with the wind of culture. It is ever-evolving and never constant. Study the trends and graphs associated with your industry. Look at the track record and attempt to pinpoint where the market is going. You don't have to be privy to what your industry or target market will be doing in 10 years. You just need to know what they will be doing in the next several months. Business life is being a full time quick-change artist.

I have talked with countless business managers,

leaders, and nonprofit chiefs that sit around and wait for customers to come to them, refusing to change their approach. This is the wrong mentality. Every idea needs constant selling, every business needs consistent growth of the customer base, every business needs a continual effort to bring in new and spending customers. While it is not a good idea to abandon your base, every successful business, especially in today's cultural climate, needs a steady flow of *new* customers. It is the necessary tension between sustaining the base while growing it simultaneously. Your existing base may move away or change their habits, thus new business development is critical. Your P&L of tomorrow is depending on new business today.

Think of the most recognized brand in the world, McDonalds. Even with their perceived lack in quality, they remain at the top of recognized brands across the globe. When you drive down the interstate anywhere in the world, what company advertises on the most billboards? McDonalds! Why? Because they understand that they have to constantly introduce new customers to their brand.

The most successful stories of our generation include businesses that have successfully generated cult-like followings and have a conscious action plan for incorporating you into their domain. Think Starbucks and Chipotle.

Ask yourself, "Am I willing to do what it takes in the lean times, in order to truly flourish when success comes?" *Think outside of the box.* Before you start with planning your business, think about how you are going to constantly reach new customers. How can you directly communicate with the audience that is most likely to purchase your products? This, of course, requires you to fully identify your *target customer*. You cannot cast a broad net in hopes to reach your catch. You have to learn who you want to reach and reach them in a way that agrees with how they receive it. This process can be difficult to assess, but it is a necessary step to finding success. My aim here is not to unpack a 12 step marketing plan. Firstly, because such specifics are not the intention of this book and second, every marketing plan is bespoke and changes depending on the client, the market, the trends, the location, and the end goal. Nevertheless, my hope is that you are spurred to think about marketing sooner rather than later. Lead generation should begin before you ever incorporate.

Ask questions like: How old is my target customer? What kind of car do they drive or clothes do they wear? What are the current general and generational interests of that customer? What is their current employment and financial situation?

These questions and more will lead you to effective and efficient marketing. I have seen too many business owners throw money away because they refuse to answer these questions in the pursuit of new customers.

There are many examples of successes in the modern era that have made an art of creating an almost cultish following of consumers as their customer base. Chipotle, Starbucks, Disney, and more have created an army of evangelist consumers that will defend the brand until death, even considering great missteps by many of these brands.

Get creative. I realized that my cash flow was thin and I made the trek across the street to the bookstore. Later I heard that Mike and the bookstore had a 20+ year relationship with Burger King to give away a Whopper Jr. to students returning their books for cash. I was asked on several occasions how I was able to get the manager to consider an alternative to the current agreement. I'm not fully sure, but he did, and we had our first of many corporate clients on our side. It all started with a short walk across the street. Before new customers would enter those doors—I had to exit them. Don't wait behind a cash register for your next customer. Meet them where they are.

CHAPTER FOUR

HITTING OUR STRIDE

OFTEN, YOUR FIRST year in business is more about surviving than it is thriving. Nevertheless, Mark Twain said, "The secret to getting ahead is getting started." We most certainly got started. Through a whirlwind of events we finally made it through one year. By the end of it, I was able to reflect on a full cycle of how our business ebbed and flowed throughout the calendar year. Christmas and the time leading up to it was steadily busy. We would hit spurts of growth and upticks here and there, but Valentines Day, hands down, was reliably our top producing day of the year. We had to learn how to organize well for that holiday every year. We got better as each year we faced higher demand and volume.

We committed to studying the business and the dessert industry as a whole. With the economic challenges of 2008 and 2009, we really had to operate in a *lean way*, particularly with labor. Business has a way of exposing our tendency to overestimate how much we know. The Dunning-Kruger effect is a common psychological phenomenon which basically states that, "The less you know about something, the more you *think* you know about it. Yet, the more you lean in and begin to learn about something, the more you realize you don't know much at all."

It's very easy to look at the cookie business, for example, and think, *It can't be that difficult. You just source the ingredients, open the doors, and fire up the oven!* The truth is, the more you peer in and discover, the more you realize processes need to be refined, studied, and executed with more detail than you could have ever imagined.

For example, we learned that our ovens were 26 steps from the ordering station—which was way too far. Our Cookie Designers would take the order, select the dough and mix-ins, mix it up on a cutting board, scoop the mixed dough onto a baking sheet, and walk at least 26 steps to the ovens for baking. This inefficiency also meant that they would return seven minutes later to retrieve them when they were done. After analyzing this process we moved the baking ovens to be located right behind the Cookie Designers to maintain engagement with customers and not break conversation. Connecting to every customer was key to our success. We wanted to maintain conversation with any customer that wanted it, as well as be accessible to anyone needing assistance. This made it easy to translate our expectations to our team, all in an effort to build our own cult-like following.

We always made time to hear the stories that customers would bring into the shop. Businesses often outweigh their *presentation,* when in fact, sometimes it's less about your ability to *present* and more about your ability to *listen.*

Beyond that, we developed a pre-order process and made a board that would keep orders organized to virtually eliminate miscommunication and order misses in our operation. We smoothed out our cash wrap strategies and developed scripts that our Cookie Designers would study. We role played in our staff meetings to ensure all team members were comfortable with the ins and outs. We added more ovens, high capacity mixers, and display cases to meet customer demands that we saw as trends in our day-to-day.

In all honesty, as a business owner you don't have to run around with a solution looking for a problem in your company. The customers will tell you what to fix. You just have to listen. A customer complaint is not the time to be defensive and argumentative. It's a time to learn and glean insight from within the noise. How can you leverage their issue to improve your business?

I loved this early season of growth and upgrades. While we did not get everything perfect, we kept a posture of learning every day. We learned many things that didn't work and more things that would, as a result of this posture.

You may be asking yourself, "What is the key to success?" Believe me, if I had that knowledge I would be a rightful genius. While we might point to pithy statements on the subject and debate the recipe for success all day, I have learned one irrevocable that applies everywhere: *learning is earning.*

Looking back at our early years as a company, learning not only enabled the business to start, but allowed it to be sustained. The more we were willing to listen to our customers, the more success we found in our business. There is a direct correlation between hearing out your customers and clients and gaining loyal patrons. Business owners are often defensive when a customer makes a recommendation about their offerings. I know business owners who developed a script to answer these suggestions because they hear them so often. If you hear a complaint multiple times, from multiple people, chances are they may be onto something. Not only that, but it is estimated that for every one customer complaint that's brought to you, seven other people noticed the same issue but simply didn't bring it to your attention. Think of a complaining customer as a spokesperson for areas that need growth. This will revolutionize your tone and approach to them.

Early on, we realized some customers didn't have time to wait for custom cookies and needed *ready to go* options. We did this and it became an instant success. Guests would come in and buy cookies by the dozen to take to the office or gift to a new mother or to celebrate a special occasion. This recommendation from our customers vastly benefited our business and incrementally increased our revenue. Our niche approach to custom cookies allowed early success. From that success, we were able to branch out and offer pre-prepared cookies, which was a non-niche, traditional sales model. If you start in a unique niche, you are able to grow and expand your business horizontally with added offers and products.

Later on we began hearing murmurings that we should do bagels. Let me make a statement you've probably not read in a book before: bagels are complicated. But, we kept hearing it so we did a test run that lasted several months. While the stock was complicated to maintain, we never sold them all and demand was low. The variety was never enough for the customer requests and ultimately we did away with them. Nevertheless, we tried. Many years later we kept hearing about doughnuts and we tried them also, but again, the demand was low. Fortunately, having an existing model that worked allowed us to run experiments with new ideas without costing us our core business. Trial and error is not only a reality when starting businesses, but it's a reality as you own and operate a successful business.

In fact, trial and error within working companies has led to remarkable innovation. Jeff Bezos once boldly remarked, "Our success at Amazon is a function of how many experiments we do per year, per month, per week, per day." And this is not just relegated to the tech space. Restaurants and retailers will offer new products or re-arrange displays slightly to gather data and determine if more investment in that area is called for. Experimentation is the epitome of forecasting trends and capitalizing on customer habits.

The best request we received from a customer was for ice cream to be added to our offerings. The pairing of cookies and ice cream certainly was not invented by us. Nevertheless, we ran an experiment and started incorporating ice cream into our menu and it was a huge, almost instant success. This led to a corporate relationship with a big name retailer of ice cream that proved to be very successful for us and for them. It occurred simply because customers brought my attention to a perceived need and we met that need with excellence.

In my years of operating businesses of all sizes I have heard some really good ideas, some of which I incorporated and some that I could not. The customer is not *always* right. Yet, when they are, and you listen and act, it could become your next highly profitable branch of business.

Cultivating Community

You need brand ambassadors. You need *buy in* guests that love what you do and recommend you at every opportunity. My recommendation is simple: always treat the customer with respect, friendship, and provide a good product.

We created a loyal following before most everyone in our area had even tasted our cookies. This was the result of faithfully developing relationships with our friends and neighbors in the community. This is a principle that I continued with every unit we opened. I would spend time at city offices, drive thrus and connect with people along the way. Cultivating a sense of community was critical. Now, this concept may not be as pertinent if you're an industrial manufacturer or a freight broker in a small office. Nevertheless, for businesses with face-to-face interaction with customers and patrons, developing a sense of community is non-negotiable.

Some of the best money I ever spent was on a wrapped "Cookie Mobile" that had Crumb & Get It branding on it from the top to the bottom. We purchased a Kia Soul and had it wrapped with images of our cookies, which advertised our ability to cater events, our social media, and eventually the opportunity to franchise. Everywhere I went in that car people wanted to know all about Crumb & Get It. In fact, I sold franchises from people seeing that car on the road. It produced better returns than any other marketing that we did. It was a flashy design and we even got invited to be the official dessert of the Virginia Tech Hokies pre-game, broadcasted nationally on ESPN.

We had come a long way from lost and bankrupt to operating a thriving business, but we still had a long way to go. Our lives were in a continual cycle of adapting, changing, and evolving. Change can be very difficult to navigate. Most people do not like to experience an excessive amount of change. Some shifts are easy, like painting a wall, moving the couch, or organizing a closet. Other changes are more drastic, costly and bear bigger consequences. Change is the great equalizer because no matter who you are, what money you make, how old you are, or what class you fit into—change is inevitable.

The Bible has much to say about change, particularly in helping us to understand that even though change may be inevitable, the Lord walks with us through these changes. The beautiful reality is that while our personal worlds are changing, God Himself is not! Malachi 3:6 states, *"I am the Lord, I change not."* The New Testament echoes this as well, stating, *"Jesus Christ is the same yesterday and today and forever" (Hebrews 13:8).* This is a beautiful reality, because while living in the midst of constant change, we *must* be able to rely on the stability of a God who doesn't.

One of my favorite places in scripture is a reminder that God goes with us through these seasons of shifts, and is not surprised by our road twists and turns. He is patient in His waiting for our coming to Him. Peter said, *"The Lord is not slow in keeping his promise, as some understand slowness. Instead he is patient with you, not wanting anyone to perish, but everyone to come to repentance" (2 Peter 3:9).*

Many times I have fallen off course and turned around only to realize I was in no way pursuing God. Then I would have the audacity to ask why He wasn't making this journey with me. Of course, that is not the case, but it can feel that way at times and has for me.

I find comfort in knowing that He is patiently awaiting my return, in repentance, to Him. My personality thrives when I run ahead with every idea because my creative juices are always in hyperdrive. Sometimes I enthusiastically run right out of His will. While our loving Heavenly Father may allow my distraction for a time, He waits patiently for me to return into His will.

Do not doubt the importance and relevance of God in your plans. He is concerned with every detail of your life and longs for you to be in full pursuit of Him, whether that is in the ministry or in the marketplace.

Some change is not by choice. Kelly and I have been forced into a corrective course many times in our marriage. In some cases we have adapted well and in others, change has devastated us. All in all, the most valuable assets we had during these times were our friends, family, and patrons at Crumb & Get It. When we needed honesty, they gave it. When success was to be celebrated, they offered it. When we needed support, they offered encouragement and guidance.

Learn to listen to your customer base. Be open and willing to hear potential improvements that come from your friends. This is where you will find your stride, and ultimately, *success*. All businesses should be able to adapt to the rapidly changing environment of culture and tastes. Many business owners create something, but are unwilling to change it, counting the cost too high. In reality, the cost of staying the same is too high in the long run. Make a commitment to be flexible in order to see the highest probability of success, especially within the first few years of being in business.

Think now about what your response will be to constructive criticism and what filters will you use to gauge those comments. Some will be great successes and some will not. Know that at every opportunity you are growing as a leader and as a company. With this mindset, you will see that there aren't any failures, only learning opportunities.

CHAPTER FIVE

COMPLACENCY AND COMFORT

KEEPING MULTIPLE PLATES spinning at once has always been my forte. After the first cookie store was opened and operating smoothly, my family and I had a brief stint in Alabama for ministry. Balancing these two worlds has been my reality for the gist of my adult life. I had found favor with a church in the northern part of the state and was hired to be the Executive Pastor. It was a thriving church that was smack dab in the midst of an incredible season of growth.

They had recently moved into a brand new facility and nearly doubled in size within a short timeframe. I was brought in to execute a number of changes to alleviate the pastor from collapsing under the significant pressures of a rapidly growing church. Growth is great, but it isn't without growing pains. In church life, those growing pains often look like a lack of systems, administrative failures, and disorganized calendars.

From the onset the tasks were simple to execute. I remember the first visit I made to their incredible facility. The walls in the main office were covered in whiteboard calendars that were scratched out with arrows drawn from one side to the other, and incoherent doodles making it a complete mess. The secretary looked at me and said, "We need help." I thought to myself, *I can do this* and ended up handling this and so many other opportunities that came during my tenure there.

I developed an even deeper love for the incredible church people while in Alabama. We executed some incredible feats together that taught me about operations and how to use my people skills to accomplish things that work for the good of the organization. Basically, I was a manager of a large, multifaceted organization that operated with a CEO and the accountability of a board of directors. While not always easy, I found success in those days and some of the best stability in my adult life.

We were loved very well by the church in Alabama. Ministry in the south means striking a unique balance between warm hospitality and authenticity. Many of the relationships we built during this time remain the closest friendships we have many years later.

One such relationship was from an adopted grandmother to our girls. Ms. Sue came into our lives at a particularly trying time for our family. Our younger daughter was a newborn at two weeks old and our older daughter contracted the dangerous H1N1 flu. We were scared for both girls and there was much news in those days about the potential for this type of flu to be deadly, especially for newborns.

We worked to quarantine the girls away from each other and had been doing all we could to protect our family. Unfortunately, this meant we had not spent much time out of the house for several days when we got a knock on our door. It was Ms. Sue with a load of groceries and a friendly conversation. This offered a much needed reprieve and introduced us to what it meant to live in the deep south. This act of kindness has given us a lifelong friend and Ms. Sue is an essential part of our family, even now.

This act was one that spoke to me about the importance of every relationship. In life, in business, and in ministry. No matter the size of the organization, the people are the heartbeat. I may have been juggling the systems of a large organization but the day-to-day acts of kindness from the people were the motor behind it all.

Kelly has always been ready to dive in any depth that I could dream up, whether that was ministry or business. With having two little hearts depending on us, we began to prioritize sound risk management and wise, careful career decisions.

While this season was comfortable, I still had the deep stirring within me to start something new, to blaze a trail for something that had never been done before. It was a constant state of discomfort, while I was content in my place, I was itching for something new, something out of the norm, something I would give my life to that would change the course of an industry. In short, I wanted to make a bigger impact. This desire has always been a part of my DNA. The single store was great, but I knew our cookie business was a model that could be duplicated.

This tension between being content with where things are and reaching for higher planes has been one of the greatest challenges of my adult life. We know and understand that biblically we are called to be content in all things (see Philippians 4). In other words, our joy, peace and satisfaction are to be derived first and foremost from the Lord Jesus, despite our circumstances. At the same time, we are called to increase (see Psalm 115:14). This means God has more opportunity, abundance, advancement, and multiplication in mind for His children, the way any good dad would! Taking new territory has been embedded in the language of the Bible and should be our directive. Living in the tension of these two things has been a routine wrestling match in my personal walk, as I'm sure many can relate with.

To navigate this balance between finding contentment in the Lord while also not being satisfied in life and career, I feel it's critical to separate our "being" and our "doing." Our *being* is about our identity and position in Christ. It is about our status as the beloved children of God. This *being* does not change and we are to find ultimate contentment in this position. However, our *doing* is more so about the work of our hands. It is a function of our labor. The Bible says, *"All hard work brings a profit, but mere talk leads only to poverty" (Proverbs 14:23 NIV)*. The work of our hands should continually become more refined, excellent, and efficient. This means we cannot *settle* or allow the sin of mediocrity to eat our lunch.

The truth is, finding balance is one of the worthiest pursuits of all. Not only have I had to do so when it comes to contentment and desire, but also with career routes. For me, I felt a constant tug of war with brewing ideas while also desiring the practicality and stability of a typical job. In all honesty, few people can maintain the dream that is set within them; most give up, favoring the comfortable route. I have certainly favored the *comfortable* at times in my life. While working normal jobs I would sometimes go back and review writings that I had produced in the past and grieve for the ideas lost on the self-forced blindness of *job security*. Perhaps it was the fear of returning to those desolate places that I had been in not so long ago or perhaps it was a concern over duplicating the business failures of my father. Regardless, I was wired for entrepreneurship and neglecting that inborn instinct simply never worked in the long run. I by no means regret many of the 9 to 5s that I've had. In fact, they can be great launchpads for an individual. I'm merely stating that for me, entrepreneurial ventures have always felt like a homecoming.

Before launching the cookie business, I had to wash the taste of failure out of my mouth, so to speak. I desperately needed to remember just who I was and understand deeply how God had wired me. I believe that God equips and builds everyone with unique wiring. You are the only *you* in the world. God designed you with a purpose already in mind. I have always taken great comfort in knowing that I have been created in His image. He knows every quirky thing about me and is interested in developing me for true effectiveness.

> *"For you created my inmost being; you knit me together in my mother's womb. I praise you because I am fearfully and wonderfully made; your works are wonderful, I know that full well. My frame was not hidden from you when I was made in the secret place, when I was woven together in the depths of the earth. Your eyes saw my unformed body; all the days ordained for me were written in your book before one of them came to be." (Psalms 139:13-16)*

It is amazing to me that in 1982, God was putting all of the pieces in place, and I was being formed with a greater purpose and nothing has been hidden from Him. There have been days where I wanted to hide. I have felt the core pain of rejection, abuse, defeat, financial ruin, and ultimate brokenness. In many ways, that too has fueled my passion and desire to find success for me and for my family.

Relentless

The discomfort of a serial entrepreneur is found in the comfort of complacency. If your heart beats like mine, in a constant state of unrest, then there will be no giving up on your idea. That, my friends, is how you identify passion. I have known many friends and colleagues who find success in being content where they are. I struggle to relate to that perspective and I have never felt true satisfaction in my career—I've always chased more. That may sound countercultural, but it has been true for me. I always look to the next idea to strive for and what has made me driven for success in business. I have never sat, rested, and not seen improvements that could and should be made.

While you may not have a take that's this extreme, you can still implement a mentality that routinely seeks improvement in the things around you. Find ways to evaluate your current processes and procedures and look for ways to improve. You may feel as though you lack this type of critical thinking and that is okay. My recommendation would be to look to your customers, or target customers, and find improvements. Whether you are in a service industry, direct, digital, hardline retail, you will have clients and they will tell you over time what to improve upon. If you are defensive rather than open, you will find a stagnant business and ultimately lack success. Be willing to listen, improve, seek to understand while making adjustments along the way.

During our time in Alabama, I implemented many of the same processes in the church that I had in business. For instance, when I arrived at the church, the books and financials were built on antiquated systems. The processes were not digitized and reports took days or weeks to generate. By the time we wrapped up our stint there, a person from the Board of Elders could approach the treasurer, ask for a report, and that document could be generated and printed off in seconds. I worked to create submission processes and request forms for the various areas of ministry. The calendar became synced up across the board and cleared of waste. I like to think that by the time we ended our tenure there, the church was administratively like a well oiled machine. It's great if a church has wonderful things happening in the sanctuary, but if it's not so wonderful in the office, the system will not hold. In 1 Corinthians 12:28, Paul placed the gift of administration in the same sentence as the gift of apostles and prophets. The Greek word for *administration* (kubernēsis) actually means to *steer the ship*. We cannot underestimate how valuable maintaining order on the back end is. Without organization, you will not have an organization.

Often, folks will separate the *administration stuff* from the *people-oriented stuff*. This is a mistake. Administrative organization has a *direct impact* on people and how they relate to each other. It sets the atmosphere, creates longevity, and sustains growth. Whether in Alabama or in other consulting-type settings, I have experienced pushback when wanting to implement new administrative systems and policy. In fact, I cannot recall a time when I didn't experience some degree of pushback. Nevertheless, as people are willing to adapt and give up old ways, they see the impact that good structure has on *people*.

In every endeavor, from nonprofit to multi-million dollar businesses, I have found that the key drivers are *the people*. The staff that you work with can make or break your business. This speaks to the importance of effective hiring and possessing a willingness to let bad people go.

As I think back to opening multiple businesses, many of which had in-house management and leadership, I always wanted to be present when key leaders were hired. I relied heavily on my savvy intuition to guide me through these very risky decisions—and it worked out.

Additionally, the customers we serve are the true center of all that we do. Dissatisfied customers or very loyal customers have the greatest impact on your success. A practice that I use to this day is making a mental note of something that is going on in the life of that customer or employee, just like I did for Cruella in those early days at the Exxon. Not in a superficial way, but with genuine sincerity. I remember that his mom just got out of the hospital, or that her kids are going through a tough time, or that they celebrated grandma's 80th birthday last week. I am convinced that these are things that yield the most business results in any organization.

While this comes naturally to me, it may not come as

naturally to you. Find a system, carry a notebook, or set a quota daily. Do what works for you—but do something to engage your customers and clients on a level deeper than a surfacy exchange. I am certain this practice will yield results for you as it has for me.

As always, this focus has helped me to remember that I too have been in their shoes. I too have experienced loss and success and it has always meant a lot to me when a leader remembers where they came from and speaks into my value in a relatable way. People are the heartbeat of any organization. They supply the rest of the company or non-profit with what it needs to thrive.

CHAPTER SIX

TRANSITION AND SYNERGY

A FTER A FEW years of operating in our first Crumb & Get It location it became evident that we had outgrown our space and with some encouragement from our landlord, by way of crippling rent increases, we made the decision to go another route and pursue another location. It was during this season that I took on my role in Alabama as well as some other consulting roles. While I don't regret that season, there is no doubt that time and attention are limited resources and when you focus on one thing, it puts the others in peripheral vision.

Admittedly, the cookie business had occupied my peripheral vision for a little while. There has been much research done on the Labor Statistics data on when and why small businesses fail. For instance, Fundera Finance found small business failure rates to be very high, with about 50% of new small businesses failing within the first five years. Why? Well, several factors were at play. Lack of experience, insufficient capital, insufficient sales, poor management, and poor planning all had their part in the failure. However, one of the bigger killers mentioned were businesses that lacked focus and lacked the ability to adapt, which both go hand in hand. During my time dabbling in other ventures, I had allowed my focus to stray, which made the business less pliable and nimble.

The result of my diverted attention was that I was resting on my laurels on the cookie business side of things. I was not giving Crumb & Get It the attention it needed. No one will ever love your business as much as you, so if you yourself are not giving it tender love and care, others will not either. We left Alabama and made our way back to Virginia to give our store another shot.

After a time of transition we set our sights on a new spot, reopened in a neighboring town and began the process of rebuilding the brand and regaining the trust of our loyal customers. This transition gave us an opportunity to introduce new menu offerings, including handmade cupcakes that were an instant success. Additionally, we made a permanent spot for our ice cream cooler which was more accessible for our Cookie Designers and it was more visible to our guests. If they can see it—they're more likely to want it. There is a reason why every big box store in America has a checkout aisle lined with small, easy to grab items. An incredible sum of money is spent annually on these impulse buys.

When we first began, we were living, and dying, by the idea that we needed to do one thing and to do it really well. While this was a solid start, things like ice cream, and cupcakes proved that we could do more than one thing well—and in a very profitable manner. Singularity is a good principle, especially when starting, but we must always be willing to evolve while not abandoning our core drivers in the process.

The biggest factor in our location change was the opportunity to totally rework our store footprint to maximize our square footage and to actually do more with less room. We were much closer to the original concept by this time and I was much happier with the look, from a design standpoint, once we made the transition.

I gained understanding of critical business considerations in the move as well. I meticulously analyzed costs and revenue per square foot, peak staffing, operational efficiency, waste reduction, seasonal changes to maximize profitability, margin product mix, and dramatically improved our bottom line as a result. Some of this success was found in vendor selection and negotiation. If a business is like a baby, then certain aspects of its care will get easier over time, while other aspects will become more involved and will require serious intentionality. People who lose their businesses are the people who let it coast.

Even more than these operational improvements, we found it even more important to do a better job of telling our story. As an example, nearly every finish in our re-imagined space was sustainable, locally sourced, recycled, and as a result, drastically reduced our need for newly sourced material. We wanted to make a better contribution for our surrounding environment. An unintended consequence was that this effort greatly reduced our build-out expense and really resonated with our target customer base. This would end up being a key point of interest for potential franchisees.

I am convinced that we could have improved on communicating this mission and fully told this story of sustainability. But, the impact was we gained a clear vision to be eco-friendly in our building construction practices in every unit we built from then on.

I personally built the fixturing using the finish carpenter skills that I had developed over time, and that my dad had questioned so long ago. I found it very satisfying to complete work like this, somehow attempting to prove my value once again. I loved this work. I traveled the area's thrift shops and lumber yards looking for the perfect materials to work my magic and develop something beautiful. My preference was solid wood doors and windows with plenty of history. All along the way I would tell our story to every merchant and vendor knowing that anyone could be a potential customer and friend for Crumb & Get It Cookie Company. I like to think it was a stroke of genius, but it was more likely to be the result of a few years of learning some hard lessons and knowing what drove our business to success.

I was adamant about design choices, to the point

where even those close to me would give up before its completion. I would work tireless hours making the perfect finish from the raw materials. I remember the sense of pride I finally was able to allow myself to feel when I stood back and saw the final product.

This process had a deeply spiritual component for me. It was liberating to know that I could accomplish something knowing that most would have doubted my ability to see it through. I spent much time in prayer during this process knowing that God had something that He wanted to reveal to me. This was yet another moment where I would truly understand what it meant to be loved by my Creator. Romans 8 reverberated in my mind:

> *"Who shall separate us from the love of Christ?*
> *Shall trouble or hardship or persecution or famine*
> *or nakedness or danger or sword? For I am*
> *convinced that neither death nor life, neither angels*
> *nor demons, neither the present nor the future, nor*
> *any powers, neither height nor depth, nor anything*
> *else in all creation, will be able to separate us from*
> *the love of God that is in Christ Jesus our Lord."*
> *(Romans 8:35,38-39)*

Just as Paul had experienced the pain that came from being ridiculed and imprisoned, I too was in my own prison. I lived in the prison of the self-doubt my father had pressed upon me. I lived with the shame and resentfulness that the abuse from my childhood and teenage years brought. I lived in bondage, even bondage that I had created for myself, the bondage of sin.

This was my time to finally be freed from all of those chains that had bound me for so long. I turned it all over to God and allowed Him to finally begin to heal and mend those broken places in my life.

Creating new things out of old things is what God specializes in. As I repurposed old materials and gave them new life in our enterprise, I sensed God was doing those same works in my heart. He can do the same for you too. If you find yourself in the place of pain, whether self-inflicted or imposed by others, there is room at the Cross for you. His sacrifice on that fateful day more than 2000 years ago marked your full and complete redemption. Admittedly, I have to find my way back to that Cross quite often. Old memories come flooding in, suggesting to me that I am not enough or that I am a failure. The truth is that I *am* enough. Not because of *me,* but because I have an advocate, sitting at the right hand of God working on my behalf, seeking my ultimate good, praying for me: His name is Jesus Christ!

We began to attend a new church near the shop. We had been going for a few weeks when the pastor gave an invitation to come forward if you needed to hear from the Lord. Kelly and I both looked at each other simultaneously and made our way to the front of the church with several others. New seasons require fresh words, and we were hungry to hear from God about where we were.

A lady met us at the altar and told us a story of a glass maker that found broken shards on the ground, but identified their usefulness. He picked color by color and shape by shape until a beautiful stained glass picture was formed. She told us that this is how God sees our life; that God was picking up our pieces and creating something beautiful. He indeed was. We didn't know the full extent of what that was, but we trusted His plan. We had never met that woman before that moment and to my remembrance never saw her again. It truly was a word from the Lord.

Will you allow Him to take the *old you*, the mess, and begin to create something wonderfully new and beautiful with your broken pieces?

The Power of Partnership

Another unforeseen benefit of the move was that we ended up two doors down from a very popular restaurant and bar that had late hours much like we did. The match proved to be one of our best strategies up to this point. The owners had a passion for partnering and I jumped right in with them at the first invite. *Never* underestimate the power of partnership. Ecclesiastes 4 famously describes two as being better than one. In other words, on our own we have limitations—we have a ceiling. Yet with partnership, we gain superpowers. In the business world we call this *synergy*. With synergy, one plus one does *not* equal two. Instead, one plus one equals three. In other words, when our powers are partnered, we can do more together than we could on our own. I knew these restaurant owners were sharp operators with a wealth of information developed from years of success and failure.

I found our conversations to be refreshing, and they always laced their stories with an incredible number of expletives. I grew to love and respect these ladies and their insatiable appetite for success. They liked me and often told me so. They had the best burgers in Virginia. The first time I sat in their restaurant I was enamored with their ability to tell their story and their incredible ability to gather people. For one thing, they were always on the floor, with their team, sharing laughs and wings with their patrons. Their approach was one I wanted to imitate. Their beef was locally sourced and they took chances on local unknown breweries to put on tap, recommending it to their loyal fans, and building a mutual trust. The atmosphere was what you would expect at the intersection of good times and good friends. Everyone called them by their first name. Sharkey's in Radford, Virginia is where I learned to become the figurative mayor of my circle much like these ladies that I had come to respect deeply.

Together, we developed a little system where each guest check from their restaurant had our logo, concept, and pictures on the reverse side and included a 10% off coupon if they came in within an allotted time frame. Additionally, kids ate free on Tuesdays. Naturally, we did a free kids scoop of ice cream in tandem. It was a match made in Heaven.

We often spend so much time making excuses and battling our potential partners that we are blind to the success that a relationship with them could bring. What if your competition is not competition but a company you could partner with for mutual benefit?

I gleaned much from this partnership with Sharkey's that had been cultivated. I learned quickly to step in time with the ebbs and flows of what they were doing. It helped that the owners and managers were always willing to partner and offer a helping hand every time we approached them. While it was not the same sort of partnership as the Virginia Tech Bookstore—the principle was the same. We locked arms with businesses in proximity for mutual benefit. Early in your business, whether it's retail or otherwise, make a commitment to explore partnership with those in proximity. If a business is hesitant, offer a trial period or set a minimum level of engagement so risk is low on all sides. Do what you can to work *with* your business neighborhood—not against it.

In both of our first ventures the local college students were our primary foot traffic patrons. In the summer the college kids would leave town and leave a void for us to fill. We worked several summers and saw decent success with ramping up our catering business through those months. One of the ways that our friends helped us was to let us add on our raw materials to their food order for the week so that we could meet the minimum caseload for delivery. In the food world, your vendors need a certain dollar amount for purchases to justify bringing a truck to you. In a mom and pop setting with only desserts, this can prove challenging, but we were insistent on bringing the freshest ingredients to our customers and Sharkey's helped us with that. Tagging on to their truckloads could not have happened without an initial step forward. A simple visit, a handshake, and a friendly introduction wound up saving us enormous headache and operating costs in the long run.

With the lessons learned and improvements made in our operational expenses, we experienced some genuine breathing room in the business. These improvements allowed us some extra working capital to explore new avenues and opportunities. Basically, we were able to do more with less. This ingenuity was birthed out of necessity due to a restrictive budget in the early days of the company. Later, we would incorporate these same principles in our franchisee's operations, greatly increasing their likelihood of success. These lessons proved to be invaluable in the training process as we looked ahead to expansion.

Use What You Have

Bringing in outside capital can certainly be a boost to a business and afford the venture some slack to try new things. Yet, not everyone has this luxury. In fact, very few startups do. As a result, bootstrapping new ideas is necessary. This means you build something new from materials and resources that are already available at your disposal. It is sort of like MacGyvering in the business world.

A number of companies have found success with this model. For instance, in the year 2000, Ben Chestnut and Dan Kurzius had a design consulting business. It was small, tidy, but had no chance for extreme success the way it was. Their clients began asking for e-newsletters, but at the time, creating them was a tedious process. So, he and his team worked to create a better way to design email newsletters, and as a result, MailChimp was born.

More than 20 years later, the co-founders' bootstrapped startup business is estimated at a value of more than $10 billion. How did they pull this off? They simply worked within the restraints of their existing design firm, treating MailChimp as an expansion that eventually grew beyond what they could have hoped or imagined. Restraints are not the enemy. In actuality, they can be your friend!

Find ways to innovate, dream, and expand while working with what is already there. Some are cash strapped before they open their doors, which can be very discouraging in the midst of what should be an exciting time. You have made a plan, you have budgeted for your needs, and you have executed your plan only to run out of steam before you open the doors.

I have stood with many business owners at ribbon cutting ceremonies where I was concerned for their physical, emotional and mental health. No matter how grueling the process of starting something new, we must never neglect the importance of *you*. Without you this new venture would be nothing anyway.

There are always opportunities to dig in and build your business, even with little cash flow. Begin to brainstorm now, and plan what some of your actions will be when and if you reach this point. What relationships will I lean on? What partnerships can I build now that can prove to be valuable in a time of need? What can I find joy in during the days when things are not as positive? These must all be part of the plan from the beginning. Learn to ask questions and find answers to those questions in the resources that you have at your disposal.

Did you know that God Himself has bootstrapped much of creation? In Genesis, the Bible describes that God *created* the heavens and the earth. However, in the Hebrews, there are actually two distinct words used to describe *create*. One use of the word *create (bara)* means to make something from nothing. The other word for create *(asah)*, means to make something from existing matter. For instance, when He created the heavens and the earth, He did so from scratch. Yet when He created man, He *formed* this being from existing material. Funny as it sounds, you and I are bootstrapped creatures! How much more should we be willing to bootstrap ventures in our lives and work with the material and resources that God has placed before us?

Limited resources and resource restraints provide an

opportunity to innovate and is a place where we can get creative to find success. An abundance of working capital can actually cause businesses to become wasteful, sloppy, and can kill creativity. Some of the best, and most effective business strategies came from times where I was *forced* to innovate. Ask yourself: What paths are you forging? What are your limitations and how can I circumvent them? Who will be my partners in this season of innovation?

My best recommendation for startups is for you to think through every relationship connection to your business. It is, perhaps, the most critical step in bootstrapping anything. Be brave enough to better yourself through relationships with business owners, vendors, real estate professionals, church leaders, and city officials. Many business people have adverse relationships in these channels and wonder why the community is not supporting their efforts. Some of our biggest brand ambassadors were local police and city officials.

There was a time when we had some renovations that required a sign off from the city planners because we were in a historic building within the city limits. I walked into the planning office, which we had been in many times, and the administrative assistant walked us right in for an immediate meeting with the Planner who signed off on our plan in minutes. Of course, we came knowing what we would do and adhered to the requests set forth from the department, but I knew of other businesses that had waited months for approval. We had an existing relationship with the staff and the Planner, and that led us to success and an expedited process.

Later, we were building a store in Fredericksburg, Virginia and our contractor was having trouble getting plan approval and the franchisees were at an impasse. The city had a reputation for delaying efforts of smaller businesses like ours. Our solution was to bake cookies and make our way to the planning office to see what we could accomplish. We gave the goodies to the staff out front and we waited for the city building official. We had a meeting, allowed him to outline his expectations, assured him of our common interest in doing it right, and left with a signature of approval to start. People are not only the heartbeat of an organization, but they are the hands and feet of it also.

CHAPTER SEVEN

A CONCEPT EVOLVED

A S WE CONTINUED on our path and found our footing through some challenging discoveries, we also found some breathing room to assess and analyze our current offerings. We continued to find areas where we could diversify our menu to appeal to a larger customer base. Cookies would always be #1 but we had equipment, resources, and capacity to do more than what we were currently offering. The cookie category always accounted for about 60% of all sales in the store after our diversified menu was implemented.

By incorporating a more versatile menu without overdoing it on raw materials, we were able to create some innovative offerings. The aforementioned full cupcake line that was developed created a more loyal following and opened us up to a broader market. We remained committed to only real, in-store production in small batches which was difficult in situations where the client needed larger quantities such as weddings or parties. It was not unusual for a client to request 500+ cupcakes or cookies that would require intensive pre-planning and precise execution as we were still abiding by our fresh-made, no preservative principles. It was common practice that we would work all night to prepare fresh offerings for next day events.

The concept of making your raw materials is a key component of most business models, particularly in food. Have you ever noticed how many things Taco Bell can make with just 6-8 ingredients? They simply put the same recipes in different shells, or bowls, making their basic rice, meat, cheese, and sour cream appeal in a different way to different guests. This was an early observation for me that we had quite a bit of success implementing. The only difference for us is that we had basic raw ingredients on site that could easily be adapted into more product offerings. You can make a whole bunch of things from flour, sugar, eggs, butter, and milk.

I had observed my father through the years, constantly adding diverse offerings within the same categories that he was working in. Small additions could yield very positive results for the bottom line. This can be implemented throughout any business or ministry landscape and yield great results. Sometimes you don't need new materials. You need the same materials, utilized in new ways, to produce novel outcomes.

Over the course of time we added quirky apparel that

would appeal to our own target demographic. This strategy usually came with a high up front cost, but we sold through quickly and made the offering 'limited' to create higher demand. Shirts, hats, themed cooking gear, and more performed very well for us both in store and online. These items were more of an impulse buy, most commonly at checkout, and typically had higher margins. These things also created better results in our key performance indicators such as items sold per transaction, and higher tickets.

Sometimes broadening our offerings yielded more results than we were initially considering. I learned this from a deal that my dad did with Subway sub shop. He had some unused open space in a convenience store that he was trying to revive. At the time Subway shops were cropping up and doing very well. He researched what it would take to get one in the vacant space. Nearly every advisor, including the bank that financed the deal, told him it was a certain crash and burn.

"People will come in and buy from Subway and not touch anything you're selling," he was told. Their argument was that the Subway would cannibalize food sales in the store. He disagreed, figuring that the Subway would increase foot traffic, leading to sales of chips, cakes, candy and drinks in the station. Prior to Subway's entrance the inside sales were somewhere in the neighborhood of $15,000 a month. My dad figured that if he was wrong and it didn't work, the store would not take a huge loss due to the heavy volume of alcohol sales that accounted for the majority of their revenue. It was a risk, but a calculated one.

Dad put the Subway in and it opened with great fanfare. The monthly inside sales went from $15,000 to $40,000 and stayed there forever. He tripled his sales by leaning into his instincts. While the business idea seemed risky, my dad understood people would buy fuel, a sub, drinks, and chips, all in one visit. It was a fairly new tactic then. Today, restaurants and sandwich shops are commonplace within gas stations. Sometimes, counterintuitive thinking is profitable thinking. This is because we are called to understand human behavior, which can often be counterintuitive and strange, frankly. Understanding business is a great attribute, but understanding people will lead to true success. Many will look out for patterns in the numbers and figures without looking at the patterns of people, as a result they stunt their own growth.

I implemented my own similar strategy at Crumb & Get it many years later. We broadened our horizons by offering free *basic* coffee. I had no idea how positive the response would be from our neighboring businesses, police officers, and regular customers. Technically the offer was with purchase, but that was not strictly enforced. Few abused the freebie and most wound up spending money in the store, figuring they had already saved a buck or two on a coffee. This created a free flow of foot traffic in and out of the shop. There were several business owners that made a stop at Crumb & Get It as part of their opening routine. We saw them everyday. We would catch up on the latest news and take some time to hear their victories and stresses of owning and operating a local Main Street business. We even threw in a little advice and help as we could. Our tribe grew exponentially through this simple offering.

I mimicked this diversification strategy in our shop often. I knew that I wanted to stay in the dessert lane and I was fearful of the specialty coffee lane because of the highly scrutinizing Starbucks generation that was also a large part of our customer base.

We had laid excellent groundwork within our catering division with many successful weddings and corporate events under our belt by this time. We had the support and relationships built with wedding and event venues, and were featured in many publications as a result. Once again leveraging the power of our relationships, we knew this area had the most feasible path forward and the greatest potential for bottom line impact.

Training is Gaining

Training and developing people can be grueling, but necessary. Henry Ford said, "The only thing worse than training your employees and having them leave, is not training them and having them stay." An essential part of our movement was constant training and support. Even after we had various levels of support management, you would still find Kelly and I in the shop re-emphasizing our standards of quality, process, and new product training. This laser-like focus made the transition to franchise expansion easy because we had been very hands-on for so long.

What are simple, feasible add-ons to your current idea that can positively impact your profitability? Using your understanding of your product margins, how can you diversify these offerings to better range your product mix for maximum impact?

Often leaders and managers expect to train someone once and they hold the employee responsible if they fail at the assigned task. Success in store operations comes from constant and consistent training and development.

Begin with a plan to hold employees accountable. Start with a solid, concise, and written training manual. Plan to have each section of the manual signed off by the employee and the trainee, this will at the very least give you common ground in holding your team accountable. This is not to say that your manual cannot be fluid, but with every update make your team sign again.

There are few things more frustrating than being held accountable for something you don't know. Similarly, it is frustrating being a leader and having an expectation that consistently goes unmet. This can all be resolved with a true look at what your initial and ongoing training looks like. Unfortunately, we cannot simply write a handbook and give an employee the binder, leaving them alone to figure it out. It requires in-person training, time, and explanation.

As an aside, in my many years of experience across

several iterations of business, I have found that employees love and appreciate fair accountability. They may not like it in the moment, but they respect that everyone is held to the same standard. Other employees look on and respect that you, as the leader, will make good on the promises outlined in your manual. If you fail to do that in a timely way, your credibility will be quickly lost, which is hard to recover from. In those cases where a manager is extremely lax and laissez faire, employees struggle to contextualize you as a leader. This will ultimately be felt by the end customer and can cost you your business.

While working in another setting later in my journey, a team I was with was asked to identify what the top three traits of their leaders were that they admired. At a near unanimous rate, "fair" and "consistent" were the top choices.

Let this feedback inspire some self-reflection in you. Ask yourself if you can be *fair and consistent* in the heat of the moment, when all hell breaks loose and it's fight or flight in your operation. List any possible scenario that you can think of and *predetermine* your response. Review and adjust it often to reflect your current operation and employee base.

Often we set out to represent Christ in the marketplace and we are to represent Him above all. The scriptures state, *"We are therefore Christ's ambassadors, as though God were making his appeal through us. We implore you on Christ's behalf: Be reconciled to God"* (2 Corinthians

5:20). Paul also wrote, *"Follow God's example, therefore, as dearly loved children and walk in the way of love, just as Christ loved us and gave himself up for us as a fragrant offering and sacrifice to God" (Ephesians 5:1-2)*.

I believe that if you can't reconcile this position in your heart you may face a harder road later. There is no problem with letting your faith shine through in your operation—and you should. The problem occurs when inconsistency sets in and team members are not sure if they are going to get their Christian boss or a tyrant boss on any given day. Commit to be an imitator of Christ, who lovingly discipled and trained His team tirelessly. He did not leave them on their own but stuck close, ultimately desiring to ensure their success in the task that God had for them. Your mission is no different. Evolving your concepts is not merely shifting your product offering, but shifting your employee training and team-member guidelines as needed. If you, as a leader, remain adaptable and flexible, your employees will see the example and often duplicate that example.

CHAPTER EIGHT

THE POWER OF A MOMENT

IF YOU WANT something done, give the task to the busiest person. Why? Because busy people know how to manage a million things at once and will find a way. As our cookie business grew, we had felt the weight of busyness on more than one occasion. On one particular morning at Crumb & Get it, we were preparing goodies for one of the largest events that we had ever done. The order was for 1,100 cookies, each with hand molded chocolate monograms, wrapped in wedding foil and tied in a decorative wedding cinch bag. Much of this was arranged and prepared in the weeks leading up to the event, but we had no choice but to wait until the night before to put all of the final pieces together.

The plan was to work in shifts, rotating responsibility through the night to ensure the treats were done and delivered on time. In addition, our kids were young and needed to be taken care of. Kelly would take the late shift and I would come in early the next morning to finish the job.

I arrived at the shop around 7 a.m. to relieve Kelly. The town was quiet and still, but I noticed there were a lot of police in the downtown area. I was unsure why. Kelly slipped out to make her way home to shower and rest.

An hour of diligent work passed. It was time to open the doors to the public for the day. I unlocked the front doors and a young lady was waiting there to get in.

"Hello, I represent President Barack Obama and Vice President Joe Biden."

I knew that Biden was planning to visit a neighboring town, but I was unaware of his plans to visit Radford on his way through. She told me that Joe Biden was taking a small detour on his journey into a political event at Virginia Tech. None of that mattered though, because she presented an offer. She described a scenario in which Biden would stop in and have an ice cream in *our shop*. It would make for a great media event with lots of exposure for our little cookie store.

What would it be like to have a major national campaign advertise our little business on a national scale? This could potentially launch us into a national market. My thoughts immediately began to consider the possible outcomes and the free advertising. What could this mean for my business?

However, there was a problem. I didn't agree with

or support the Obama ticket. In fact, a few weeks prior Obama stood on the steps of a local fire department in Roanoke, Virginia and said these words, "If you have a business, you didn't build that." Those four words, *you didn't build that,* sent a shockwave throughout America. Hardworking small business owners felt the sting of insult, delivered by a politician who had never built a company in his life. Truthfully, I was angry and hurt by the statement. Kelly and I had put everything we had into our small business. We worked day and night. We slaved and scraped to get by. We hired and paid employees faithfully. We tried our hardest to meet customer demands. What do you mean *we didn't build this?* I was livid at the ignorance and arrogance of the statement.

The decision was simple and on the spot I declined the invitation, informing her that we wouldn't be used for a photo-op. Crumb & Get It wouldn't be used as damage control for Obama's ignorant statements about small businesses. We refused to assist the tainted Democratic brand. "This will be career suicide. This will bring a ton of publicity to your business," she said, in an attempt to convince me.

"No thank you," I said.

Outside, I watched as she scrambled with her team to make adjustments to Biden's trip through town. They wound up moving Biden's stop down to a shop that has never been heard of again, and frankly, didn't receive the national exposure that the Biden aide had promised. Biden stopped there within twenty minutes. He never entered the building, didn't buy anything, he kissed a few babies and headed to Virginia Tech. He was gone as fast as he came. It was over. Back to work.

Following that unusual surprise, a friend who owned a dress shop down the road came in to get her morning coffee. I casually mentioned the ordeal with the Biden representative. Nothing seemed to come from the conversation. She left the shop and we went back to our big order.

A few minutes passed and we got a call from a news anchor for our local CBS affiliate out of Roanoke, Virginia, WDBJ 7. He asked if he could swing by and ask a few questions about the morning. I agreed.

It turns out, our dress shop friend had reached out to one of her friends who worked in the news industry and they connected the anchor to us. Soon after, a state trooper stopped on her motorcycle in front of the shop and made her way in. She was laughing as she came in, "The police radios went crazy over you changing up Biden's arrangements," she told us. I had no idea we rerouted the entire entourage and forced them into "unverified" space. She bought some goodies and left.

The whirlwind had begun, and I was starting to become aware of it. A group of suits walked in and they told me a similar story as the state trooper. They were Secret Service agents that accompanied Biden on the in-town leg of the tour. "We've never seen a business, much less a small business, turn down that kind of publicly," they told us. They explained that once Biden arrived where they were, they were relieved and the next security detail took over. In short, they were off-duty as soon as Biden showed up. They wanted cookies so we boxed them up and then they asked for a burger recommendation. Naturally, I sent them to our friends at Sharkey's.

We tried to keep up with the existing orders that were made prior to that day and found ourselves falling behind schedule. Kelly and I were committed to keeping our customers as the top priority. We made calls to every person and made arrangements to deliver the product to them as it may have been difficult to reach the store with all of the activity downtown. After delivering the product we headed back to the shop. Inside there was a reporter waiting to ask questions about the morning. I agreed to do an interview and the camera rolled. The station anchor said, "Would *you* turn down a visit from the Vice President of the United States?" The interviewer then picked up the piece, asking, "What happened? What followed? *Why* did you make *that* decision?"

The shot cut live to the anchor on the street who clipped my interview from earlier, provided his commentary, and led to the next news of the day. It was over and that was that.

But it wasn't.

An hour later, an interviewer came back in the shop and asked if I would do a quick follow up to reflect on the coverage. People began to flood in from all over. Some thanked me for taking a stand. There were a few supporters of the administration who pushed back, but not many. They thanked me for having the courage to stand when it would have been easy to open our doors to the V.P.

After I agreed to meet for the follow up, the anchor met me on the corner of the street where he could get a wide shot of our storefront during my comments. While we were getting set up his phone rang and it was Florida Governor Jeb Bush's office asking about the legitimacy of my story. This local anchor had worked for Fox in Florida and was well connected with Bush's political interests. He verified the story and Bush's office said they would look into it.

It was at that moment that I learned that our story had been picked up by all major cable news outlets and was being broadcast on every channel as well as on the internet. We flipped on the television in the shop and saw my face on CNN, MSNBC, Fox News, CNBC, and more. We couldn't believe our eyes. Then the phone started ringing from literally all over the world.

I don't think I fully understood the magnitude of what was happening, but I knew I would not have made the decision any differently if I could rewind the clock. As the day went on people began to line up down the street just to get into our shop. We had our usual stock which we ran out of by 2 p.m. We resorted to shaking hands and eventually closing early as a result of being inundated with customers. Guest after guest came through our doors, looking for us and cookies. There was no way for us to keep up with this kind of demand.

We saw television cameras from all over our region reporting the events of the day and shedding light on our little Crumb & Get It Cookie Company in Radford, Virginia. We went from a steady and local fan base to a nationally recognized brand in a matter of minutes.

Fortunately, we didn't forget about our bride and groom that we had worked so closely with for months to provide treats for their wedding. Kelly talked with them often throughout the day and they were very understanding of our circumstances. We returned to the shop in an attempt to get a head start on the next day and someone met us there to pick up their wedding favors and they were delivered just in time.

Later we received one of the kindest cards from the bride and groom, thanking us for making good on every promise to deliver top quality cookies to their wedding guests. I still cherish these compliments.

Standing Strong

What does it mean to work in a secular environment but maintain a Christian perspective? I will admit that it has been hard for me at times. This world no longer holds high standards, it compromises where it can, and no longer rewards ethical business practices.

I find encouragement from the story of Daniel. King Nebuchadnezzar had burned the temples in Jerusalem where Israel worshiped, compromising all security and peace. He sent for the brightest and best men from the city to be brought to him to be groomed to serve in his government. He intended to indoctrinate them in the Babylonian customs.

He wanted to teach them a new history, a new language, change their diet, and even change their names. This all sounded reasonable to some, but actually came as a huge detriment to these who had grown up worshiping the true God, Yahweh. They were told to denounce their faith to be the best in his new regime. They would have to deny God and worship a new king.

Daniel, along with some other brave men stood in the gap and refused to compromise their faith.

"But Daniel resolved not to defile himself with the royal food and wine, and he asked the chief official for permission not to defile himself this way." (Daniel 1:8)

He didn't cave on his convictions. This is the strength of a true leader. While it wasn't popular, while intense pressure mounted, while everyone else was doing it, Daniel refused to bend.

This decision was not made *in the moment*. Daniel had previously decided he would not compromise, even before he was confronted with adversity. The scripture says, "Daniel resolved..." In other words, he made the decision beforehand. Daniel knew making godly decisions in the heat of the moment was harder than having a *set* conviction. He was committed to representing God *before* he had the opportunity to compromise. When it comes to temptation of any kind, your decision to remain right needs to be made long before the temptation to cave ever shows up.

Build convictions before you are faced with adversity. When you have a grounded resolve, you will find it easier to make godly decisions. The series of events in my story underscored the importance of making my decision ahead of time. When this aide walked in, I did not have three days to weigh the pros and cons or decide what I should do. It was a snap decision, but one of conviction no less. The more you know your values and your principles ahead of time, the better decisions you can make in the heat of the moment. No amount of publicity, threat, or money can push you from that foundation.

This is an essential part of getting into any leadership position, whether in the ministry or in the marketplace. Make a resolve that you will not compromise, whatever the cost. The short term results may be unfavorable, but the long term results will lead to much greater outcomes.

What resolutions can you make now, before the pressure is on, to be on more solid footing in your ministry or marketplace leadership position? I would encourage you to write out three to five nonnegotiables for you and your business. A business will always reflect the resolve and nature of its leader.

What would you like to be known for in your community and business dealings? How can you more effectively represent Christ in every circumstance that comes your way as an operator? Who will support you and hold you accountable to operate in a strong, ethical way?

Oftentimes, regular patrons will hold you accountable for those missteps. In my years of experience, people have come to me in a loving way and said, "Chris, that decision was not the right one and I expect you to make it right." While it may be hard to hear in the moment, it was what I needed to continue to represent light in a world or darkness. This is how we live for God in a culture that opposes Him. At other times, a decision is validated and confirmed by those trusted voices near us.

In the case of the situation with Biden, my course of action had been carried out correctly and with conviction.

CHAPTER NINE

THE PUBLIC EYE

I RECEIVED A call from Mitt Romney's chief campaign media team within days. They wanted to pick up the story and use it to convey that hard work pays off and that America was built on the backs of everyday people that were willing to take the risk.

I suggested we adopt a sort of "response" idea and pitched it to them. It actually ended up front and center for the campaign that read like this, "We *did* build it," in a direct response to Obama's statements a few weeks prior. The team picked it up and carried it for months as the campaign season heated up.

The head of media for the Romney campaign began to manage our requests for interviews and helped us navigate the treacherous waters of politics that were ahead. We were getting calls at all hours of the day and night and we learned that we could trust that team as they never steered us wrong. This relationship was invaluable to us for this season.

After a long and eventful day I made a call to our food vendor for supplies and ingredients. They promised to have it all to us by mid-morning. Then I called our ice cream supplier, who loved our shop and had worked with us to develop additional offerings within our product line that complimented the current mix. They said that they too would have a delivery to us by early morning.

As an aside, many restaurateurs see their suppliers as a necessary evil. We had worked to develop valuable relationships that proved to work in our favor, especially in this moment. All suppliers had visited us by 10 a.m. and we returned to the kitchen getting our goodies back in supply. As quickly as we were making them— they were gone. There was no way we could maintain the volume of demand over these next few days. I was being pulled in all directions as the story grew in popularity. I received calls from all media outlets, from cable news to radio programs and beyond. International outlets reached out having a particular interest in the circus that is American politics.

Our contact, David Carl, from our food service company, Sysco, played an instrumental role in helping us to navigate this new season of fame. Dave had done many things for us throughout our first years in business that proved to be invaluable. He did a complete analysis of ingredients and was able to formulate a per item cost of goods sold as well as estimate a calorie count in their lab as it was then required by federal guidelines under the Obama administration. I remember looking up from the mixer and seeing Dave with cases of ingredients in hand as he made his way through the crowd.

Dave even knew where we stored everything and put it all away just as we would have. Sysco sent an army of people to help, including their regional and area manager from out of town. I am forever grateful that this team came to us as they did. Later, Sysco was able to provide excellent customer service as we grew into new markets, ensuring that raw goods that went into our products were the same from store to store. I love and appreciate the entire team at Sysco. Unfortunately, Dave had been diagnosed with a very aggressive form of bladder cancer. He fought hard but lost his fight a short time later. Before he passed, Dave came to visit us in a nonbusiness manner and we were able to thank him for always being there to support us. We offered our prayers, especially for his son who had some physical limitations also. Kelly and I were devastated when we received the news of his passing through their regional manager. I would argue that we would have not been able to succeed as we did without Sysco Dave. I still miss his jovial spirit and sarcastic approach.

Teamwork

Teamwork and dependency on others is not a new concept. One of the best examples of leadership and teamwork is found in the book of Nehemiah. Nehemiah executed one of the greatest feats that has ever been accomplished.

God placed it on Nehemiah's heart to rebuild the wall and establish the safety and security that would come with it. This was something that he would never be able to accomplish on his own. It would require superior leadership skills and a massive team with incredible continuity and support.

Nehemiah 3 reads much like a Hebrew phone book. In actuality, it tells a beautiful story of the people that came to the aid of their land and got to work. Section by section, families took on the responsibility of rebuilding the walls and gates that were in front of their homes. They each took responsibility for their section and the collective effort eventually led to the completion of the wall in 52 days.

There was a critical moment that is actually found at the end of Nehemiah chapter 2, when Nehemiah himself stood before the people and gave an inspiring speech about how they could overcome this great task and find success for themselves and for the sake of the Lord.

> *"Then I said to them, 'You see the trouble we are in: Jerusalem lies in ruins, and its gates have been burned with fire. Come, let us rebuild the wall of Jerusalem, and we will no longer be in disgrace.'"*
> *(Nehemiah 2:17)*

Once he completed this inspiring talk the people responded enthusiastically, *"They replied, 'Let us start rebuilding.' So they began this good work"* (Nehemiah 2:18).

They all agreed and committed to get to work. There are few things that can stop a team that is fully committed to the vision of the leader or the task at hand. The people around me, my family, vendors, employees, were my saving grace in this unprecedented time. I would have never survived without the support of Dave and countless others that we had spent years developing successful relationships with. We were able to build our wall and ultimately find success. Had we not pioneered these relationships prior, the business could have collapsed at the height of our national recognition.

Accomplishing this incredible work took layers of leadership that can be a clear guide for how we operate our business. In Nehemiah's example, we see leaders, managers, and workers. Knowing *how* to do the job was the accomplishment of the worker. *Ensuring* the work was being done right was the accomplishment of a manager, and *inspiring* others to do the job right was the responsibility of the leader.

These are critical pieces to consider when making your plans for business, ministry or marketplace. Knowing what kind of people you want in every position is an essential decision to make before you turn the first wrench on your business idea.

Wouldn't it be cool if every person you hired was fully committed to your vision? The quest for us as leaders is how do we inspire others to buy into our vision? Is it your presence on the sales floor? Would it be your belief in each person to achieve greatness? Could you do more than say you are interested in promoting your team, and actually promote someone?

In my experience, this is accomplished in settings where mere words are not enough. Culturally, people are done with lip service. This means that nearly every person on your team will judge your leadership by what you *actually put into practice*. Meaning, you need to *show them* more than you *tell them*. This is the true measure of effective leadership.

CHAPTER TEN

WELCOME TO THE SHOW

WE HAD BEEN in constant communication with the Romney campaign's public relations team. I had been scheduled for many television and talk radio spots. We were looking ahead to a presidential rally hosted in Roanoke, Virginia that would have appearances by local, state, and national leaders including Vice Presidential candidate Paul Ryan.

When the idea was pitched to me, I was slated to be in the speaker lineup and appear early in the program for that event. As time progressed I was moved to introduce Ryan and appear on the stage before him.

I prepared my words and was told by the campaign leaders that I had their trust. At some point, the campaign tacked on 4,000 cookies for the event to welcome guests into the rally, which was a great feat given our shop footprint and capacity.

Kelly and I had thorough FBI background checks and were ushered to a super exclusive area upon arrival where we would be one-on-one with the Vice Presidential hopeful. I prepared ahead of time by researching some of his interests so I could have something to talk about with Ryan. I determined that he was very interested in health and kept a particularly regimented workout routine, even on the campaign trail. I've always felt it is important to know your audience and prepare for any circumstance. People who do really well in conversation are generally those who can adapt to diverse interests and topics.

Oftentimes you don't have the ability to research your stance or calculate your response, but it just comes as an extension of who you are. Success comes when you are you, and you let that passion steer the way. Decide ahead of time what your values are and you will find less compromise when the moment comes.

I will never forget that handshake. We met Ryan and he talked to us like we had value, like a peer, like we had something to offer the world. We were truly amazed. After our time together the campaign pulled me aside and said that I would appear on stage with Paul Ryan and that we would walk to the podium together. This had never occurred in a rally to date. It was always an introduction then the candidate would appear and make their way to the platform. I was blown away by this. My simple but firm stand at our cookie shop had so quickly led to an unthinkable platform.

I shared my words, Paul Ryan shook my hand and stepped to the podium. His first words were, "How do you follow that?" I am forever grateful for the way he treated me and our family. Through our political dealings we encountered some interesting characters, but Paul Ryan was first class and made us feel valued.

People often won't remember what you said, but they will remember how you made them feel. Kelly and I can honestly say that Congressman Paul Ryan made us feel valued and heard. For one of my Fox News television appearances the producers of the Greta Van Susteren show sent a limousine to pick me up from our shop and drive me to the television station where I would appear live later that evening. I have never been treated with this much esteem in my life. The driver even opened and closed the car door for me.

Once the chauffeur returned to the driver seat he asked if I was comfortable and then proceeded to roll the partition window up separating me from him. "If it's ok, could you leave it down so that we can chat?" I asked.

He was baffled. This was not something that he had experienced in hauling celebrities and dignitaries around the city. I made small talk and found out about his family and his "real" job and told him that I respected his work ethic and based on what I heard, I knew he would accomplish his goals in short order. I asked him, who were his favorite people to drive for. He told me about many people that he had driven, mostly names that you would recognize, but he finally said that his favorite people to haul were professional wrestlers. By and large they were the kindest, most inclusive people that he had given rides to over many years in the business. I asked what it was that he liked so much about them and his response was simple: they made him feel *valued*.

After the rally my appearance requests increased. An interesting development was that my cell phone became inoperable for a few hours following that rally. This only occurred one other time after I had appeared on the Greta Van Susteren show on Fox News Channel.

The next few days and weeks were a whirlwind. From many radio appearances on the top talk radio shows in the country to television appearances, limo rides and more.

But I never lost sight of our little shop through it all.

The Fox News appearances were big and the viewership numbers were high, yet one of the largest influxes in business came from YouTube. A series of videos were posted by various channels, shedding light on us and the incident.

This experience solidified the importance of being online and the greater impact this would have above large national media outlets. Interestingly enough, while we had an incredible social media following, we did not have a website. This was a mistake, but we could not have anticipated this high of a demand. I threw together a quick website, mainly with our contact information. We were able to get our site live within a few hours.

This was a difficult call for me, because I like to present the very best product available. I believe it can positively or negatively impact your brand very quickly. Digital assets are one of the most critical aspects for any business seeking legitimacy. It was a lesson for me to set that innate perfectionism aside to effectively address an immediate need. As part of this build, we were able to quickly craft a simple online ordering system and test our shipping methods all around the country.

We started with our current vendors, looking for quick access to existing packaging. We worked through hundreds of scenarios and packaged up cookies to send to friends and family in other parts of the country. When we arrived on something that would work we opened up the portal on our site. And, on day one...*it crashed*... but quickly caught up to handle demand! We were now shipping all over the world from Radford, Virginia.

Additionally, the Republican National Committee had booked us to cater their counter event to the Democratic National Convention in Charlotte, North Carolina. They treated us like royalty and my two girls tagged along for the ride. I have never seen such a production before or since that assembly.

Value

In a moment of self reflection I realized that all of my life God had been preparing for this moment. There is no way I could have navigated this as smoothly as I did without the preparation that had led me to that moment. From my days at the Exxon station, through my multiple failures and attempts to earn the favor of my father and find success, through the sexual abuse of my childhood and teens, I knew how to value people, because I knew the depths of feeling like I had no value. Nothing you experience will be wasted. Your entire life is in the funnel of God and will ultimately be squeezed into a place of purpose and fulfillment.

Your time at that awful job was not a waste. That detour that cost you years will be redeemed. That divorce was not the end. The painful betrayal from a business partner won't be squandered. God will redeem and use every aspect of your life to bring you to ultimate purpose. Learn to value your past, God will redeem it. Romans 8:28 describes God working *all* things together for your good. God's ultimate recipe is that he can take a mixture of good, bad, and ugly, and still bring about *good* in the end.

One of the greatest lessons in life is that our value does not come through others. Our value does not stem from our accomplishments. Our value comes from one place, that is God the Father. If this is not our focus, we will fail to allow Him to establish us and redeem our ups and downs.

Paul writes to the church at Ephesus, *"For we are his workmanship, created in Christ Jesus for good works, which God prepared beforehand, that we should walk in them"* *(Ephesians 2:10)*. You are the most valuable thing to God. Your value is evidenced by the price He paid.

If God paid such a high price for us, *what price are we*

paying for people? Are we paying a high price to achieve a great bottom line while neglecting the very *people* we are called to serve? While perceived success in business and in life are great on their surface, nothing is worth the sacrifice of your most important ministry that is found at home.

Admittedly, I have caught myself making this sacrifice and felt the long lasting effects in my marriage and in the relationship with my kids. But, I am eternally grateful for their grace in my pursuit of what I believe God has called me to. I deeply value what Kelly has given me in this gift of trust and commitment.

A common theme in my life has been a lack of value. Fortunately, I have been blessed with an eternal optimism that has driven me to always believe that there is success on the other side of that trial. But, if I were being honest, not everything has felt like a success. Deep down I have always felt like there was always more to achieve, more to conquer, more to tackle in nearly every area of my life. I do not have the wiring that achieves and then sits on the spoils. If I achieve, I always seek to achieve more.

My encouragement to you would be to savor the moment. Always seek to learn and grow. You never know when you might need the skills you learn in these seasons in your toolbelt. This goes for life, ministry, and workplace. Value those that value you. Let God recalibrate your sense of value. As you do, you will begin to care about the things He cares about and you will lose your sense of value for the things He does not.

Keeping Christ as the plumbline for your sense of value will carry you through wild seasons. During our stint on the political scene, keeping a godly sense of value allowed us to keep the main thing the main thing. It gave us a sense of stability and confidence during a season of change and pressure.

CHAPTER ELEVEN

FINDING OUR FOOTING

GROWTH IS GOOD. Until it isn't. Declining sales are not the only thing that can kill a business. Huge spikes in sales can be its downfall also. There are a number of companies that grew so fast they could not sustain or handle the influx and ultimately caved, not because of a lack of capital, but because of a lack of capacity. For instance, Instagram is a social media platform with 1.4 billion users. Facebook, WhatsApp, and YouTube are the only social companies that beat it in terms of user count. Funny enough, Instagram could easily not exist right now. In 2010 when the company started, they offered a nice, clean photo-based alternative to the word-filled posts of Facebook and Twitter.

The platform launched and grew at an incredibly rapid rate. Within a few months they had over a million users. The problem is, this huge influx caused their app to crash. In the tech world, this is a death sentence. When new users see an app crashing consistently, they bail out and never go back. Instagram had such explosive growth that the servers could not keep up and the app went down for awhile, tainting their launch in the app store.

This sort of thing has killed a number of startups and Instagram could have easily been a statistic, had they not scrambled to patch their system and maintain users. This same sort of failure happens in businesses everywhere. Some grow so fast they have to make major capital expenditures to keep up. Then, when a downturn occurs, their inflow cannot sustain their upkeep.

When the political incident occurred, the company required vast amounts of energy and effort in order to not be crushed by the growth. As best we could tell, our business had tripled and stayed that way long after that now infamous event. We maintained a loyal following and customers remained interested in supporting us and our efforts. I found that the incredible value of our tribe kept us encouraged through the challenging and rewarding season. Many people helped us keep our heads above water. Our Alabama grandma, Ms. Sue, came and stayed in our home with our kids while we worked long hours at the shop. An employee that we had hired on a work permit many years prior came and helped us man the point of sale for months after the event. Our food service vendors, landlord, community first responders were there any time we needed them. Our friends at Sharkey's had delivered meals to us almost daily for weeks. The list goes on and on.

I believe that God had placed these people in our lives, even if they didn't know He had. Community is how we progress in life, in ministry, and in business. We owe a great debt to these friends, and more, because they saw us through when we were in need. I am reminded of the great redeeming work that Paul wrote about in Galatians. *"Carry each other's burdens, and in this way you will fulfill the law of Christ" (Galatians 6:2).*

Paul is speaking about doing good and bringing others up when he is discussing how to handle those that are bound by sin or not abiding in the Word. His message to the church was we do good *to all people.* He goes on to write, *"Therefore, as we have opportunity, let us do good to all people, especially to those who belong to the family of believers" (Galatians 6:10).*

It is in this spirit that we were on the receiving end of so much good, from within the church and from outside of the church. It was beyond explanation. Many from different backgrounds, different faiths, different races, and different political inclinations came to us in support because of a whisper from the Holy Spirit directing them.

While we had seen success outwardly, we still knew what financial struggle meant. I still felt the pain of swiping our food stamps card at the grocery store and that sting was unlike anything else. Those closest to us knew of our need, but most did not. I still had that nagging feeling of how I was struggling all these years later to truly provide for my girls without being dependent on aid from the outside.

It has always been hard for me to accept help from the outside. I feel I should be the one giving others help in times of need, rather than receiving it. I have always thought if I worked hard enough and long enough I should be able to financially prosper. I can tell you from experience that this is not necessarily the case. I know many who work very hard and still find themselves in need of help. As believers, it is our job to help those in need, even when the need isn't apparent. *"...that there were no needy persons among them. For from time to time those who owned land or houses sold them, brought the money from the sales and put it at the apostles' feet, and it was distributed to anyone who had need"* (Acts 4:34-35).

This is the church we saw in action in our story. These words describe the disciples we encountered during our hard times. This leads me to a question, "What if today's church followed this example?" It is a question that leads me to give as generously as has been given to us.

Our ability to finally free ourselves from our dependence on government support was a result of this generosity. Kelly and I rejoiced and celebrated when I called our local Community Services office to cancel our food stamps. I was thrilled to call them as soon as we were able. The nice lady on the other end of the phone said, "Are you sure you want to cancel, Mr. McMurray?" I said, "Yes, I'm sure." What a glorious victory for our family.

I never intended to be on food stamps long term, but

our circumstances were long term. Some of these circumstances were self-imposed and some were imposed on us. Either way, I was glad to make that phone call. It was as if I had received a new lease on life. I had experienced redemption in a way I could have never seen coming. I finally felt redeemed, loved, and valued in the way that God destined me to be.

Inspired by Benevolence

It was in this moment that I felt I had overcome the demons of my childhood, years of rejection and a lack of care and support. It wasn't about a mere food stamp. It was about what it represented. Being off of them meant we had stepped into a sort of *promised land* of our own. The deep guilt from the sexual and mental abuse had not only driven me, but was now something that influenced me to work hard and strive to walk into my destiny. God can take what the enemy meant for evil and turn it around for *our good*. I have determination in believing my identity in Christ and not how others value me.

I will admit it is still hard for me to accept when someone blesses our family. Maybe it is the result of years of struggle, rejection, and mental anguish. Or, it could be the result of my pride and effort to prove my worth to everyone I encounter. Whatever the case, this was one of the most profound moments of my adult life.

After this experience I vowed to always sow this seed of kindness and generosity, even if it is painful to do so. I want to be known as someone who values others more than myself just as described in Paul's letter to the church in Philippi, *"Do nothing out of selfish ambition or vain conceit. Rather, in humility value others above yourselves, not looking to your own interests but each of you to the interests of the others"* (Philippians 2:3-4).

I don't want to do so in expectation of receiving, but rather to honor my Father who has shown me much mercy...even when I didn't deserve it. I sow into others so that the harvest will be plentiful for generations to come.

This is my heartbeat and the motivation behind it, pressing me to find success in business and in ministry. It is bigger than me and always has been. The heartshift was even bigger than the financial shift in those days. We began to get letters and donations from all over the world, letting us know that we had support even as we faded out of the limelight. I felt a huge sense of relief when the media attention and scrutiny subsided and we returned to a new form of normalcy.

I felt very committed to send a response letter to every one of our supporters letting them know that these donations would go to a good cause. We developed a plan to utilize every donation for a purpose beyond the business. We meticulously donated every penny to causes such as providing cookies to our local Veterans Hospital and throwing a Christmas party for the kids in our community without discrimination of socio-economic status.

A prized memory of mine is from when we took our

girls and a few hundred cookies to an alzheimer's and dementia care unit at the VA hospital. We spent several hours singing, shaking hands, playing games and showing the people love. The nurses told us that most in the ward were forgotten and rarely visited, but we had a blast with them. On our way home we sat and cried recollecting the magnitude of the gift we had been given.

We were able to maintain this posture for many months and wove it into our DNA as a company from then on. I learned an important lesson in this time of rejoicing. It seems simple, but it's a concept that is difficult for many business and ministry leaders to grasp: it is critically important to blend family life, business and faith for the purpose of meaningful impact on others.

I have been asked often why I chose to go the route of giving rather than bankrolling our business. The answer was nonnegotiable for me; I wanted to bless others as much as God has blessed us. I will not allow someone's circumstances to change my view of their situation. I want to be the one that is reaching out a hand for the other that is struggling to get ahead. My calling is to be a blessing to others and represent Christ in the marketplace. This brings me the most joy of anything that I have ever successfully accomplished.

Learn to weave your *calling* into your *planning*. Seek the whispers of the Holy Spirit and learn to check whether you are in or out of sync with that calling. I believe He will speak to you and I know He will lead you if you seek Him.

We do have an enemy. When you begin to lean into your calling, opposition will arise. This opposition can come in many forms, be it deep financial despair, discouragement from yourself and friends or rejection from those closest to you. We must press into the Spirit and overcome this pushback.

Pray with an unwavering expectation to hear from the Lord. Pray through your pursuit and ask Him to reveal His purposes and plans for you. He is willing, and able, to blow your mind with deeper purpose and passion when you *commit to prayer.*

> *Now to him who is able to do immeasurably more than all we ask or imagine, according to his power that is at work within us, to him be glory in the church and in Christ Jesus throughout all generations, for ever and ever! Amen. (Ephesians 3:20-21)*

My hope for you is that He will begin to shift your focus from only receiving to also being a blessing to others. This is what drives successful business. Solomon described that *"He who waters, will himself be watered, the generous person will prosper" (see Proverbs 11:25).* Christ echoed this in the New Testament, stating, *"It is more blessed to give than to receive" (Acts 20:35).*

Some of the most prominent brands that find success are ones that are committed to the spirit of giving. From coffee companies who commit to provide jobs for underprivileged families to shoe companies that commit to give footwear to children in need. These are the companies that will be the most sustainable through seasons of change.

Always drive yourself to remember your *why*. This is where you will find ultimate fulfillment in your God-given dream. Your location, customer base, and processes will change over time, but your *why* will remain steadfast.

CHAPTER TWELVE

MOVING AHEAD

ATTENTION OPENS DOORS. Coming into the national spotlight afforded me opportunities outside of my normal domain. By this point in our journey I had spent ample time in the pulpit speaking and sharing. I had clocked hours in private consulting-related conversations. Yet I received new invites to speak in college classes and business clubs. I did this as often as I could.

One of the most common questions I got while in these settings was, "How do you define success?" Longing, young, and excited eyes would look at me expecting to say success was found in the car in your garage or the neighborhood you are privileged to move into, but I always loved throwing them for a loop with my answer: *My success is defined by how much I am able to give.*

If I am in a position to give freely then I consider that a success. I've always been generous probably to my detriment. There have been times that I have given when it has hurt my personal financial stability. I have reached deep into my pockets to support my church or a family member. Many people who find success become increasingly greedy with their tithes, time, and talents. I have always fought that tendency in the hopes that someone else might be elevated. I firmly believe that is the only reason I have found this measure of success. I can relate to Paul in that I know what it is like to have something and I know what it is like to have nothing.

I know what it is to be in need, and I know what it is to have plenty. I have learned the secret of being content in any and every situation, whether well fed or hungry, whether living in plenty or in want. I can do all this through him who gives me strength. (Philippians 4:12-13)

Memories of plenty and lack both have their places in my mind and through it all, God has allowed us to walk out on the other side with a heart of generosity. Even when I have lived in plenty I have easily been able to quickly remember my plight as a young husband relying on food stamps to feed my family. My encouragement to you would be to always stay humble and remember that it is impossible to know the true identity of the person behind the words for those you are interacting with. They may be in deep need financially, they may be contemplating how they can move on from abuse, they may look successful, but everyone needs *someone* to help them on their journey. I will always proclaim that I can do all things through Him that gives me strength. This is for everyone, especially those who are suffering now.

Finding Normal

As expected, the media frenzy faded over the next several months. Election hype dissolved and life kept moving for our family. We quickly implemented a number of offerings as a response to demand during this time. We had thousands of requests to ship our cookies around the world. We partnered with the USPS and developed packaging, tested our timing, refined our process and streamlined it all. It worked great. We hadn't tried many of these things before but leapt in head first. Never let the "we've never done that before" stop you from expanding your audience.

We had the opportunity to ship our cookies to the brave men and women serving in Afghanistan for the United States of America. We filled several orders for different outfits, but also added to the recipients based on some donations we had received.

We developed a full product line for shipping, including custom logo design packaging that companies contracted with us to ship around the world on their behalf. We made a full online store that exploded within days of it being live. We spent many more sleepless nights working tirelessly as a result of adding this offering.

Our progression and growth was always very natural and based on demands that we had experienced along the way. As things settled down for us we had several people that were very interested in franchising. The thought had crossed our minds in the past, to be sure, yet now rubber was meeting the road and we actually had people with real dollars lined up to open branches.

We followed up with our interest and began working with a consulting firm that helped us tremendously as we developed our idea into a fully scalable franchise business. We found out quickly that franchising was a grueling process filled with potential setbacks and needed professional guidance from beginning to end. We were encouraged by every person that we encountered that our idea was sound and would introduce something new into the marketplace.

We caught the attention of several competitors and worked through some challenges on copyrights and trademarks ultimately succeeding in our effort. Don't let setbacks or hindrances deter you from your dream. If your dream is easy to cave on, you may need a better dream.

In short order we had begun talks with several potential franchise partners throughout the country and even a few internationally. We went on the advice of our franchise consultants and made an effort to keep our operating units to a region that could be traveled reasonably for the time being.

A few months later we had signed agreements with franchisees in Virginia, Florida, North Carolina, and Texas.

I worked very hands on in every deal and even custom built cabinetry in the shops. I was particular about the way we wanted it to look and I had learned a lot about layout over our years in operation. I was passionate about maintaining sustainability. Kelly and I led the training for every operating unit. We traveled extensively to sell, train staff, and open units. We encountered many great people and were thrilled with our progress.

We had a laser-like focus on company development and we utilized our food vendors to develop nationwide strategies. The consistency of delivered raw goods in our shops was a big issue and we set up protocols to ensure all would be operating smoothly. We negotiated pricing that would benefit franchisees and help to yield bottom line results. We utilized our local contractor in all store development to standardize construction and save up front cost for our franchisees. Our success was built with the complete support of our partners from concept to operation. I am very thankful to have been a part of this incredible team. Things had been good so far, yet we were entering a completely new level of enterprise.

CHAPTER THIRTEEN

THE FIRES OF A NEW ADVENTURE STILL BURNED

There is no substitute for passion.

I ONCE HAD a dream that I was visiting a college friend who was battling cancer in a local hospital. His prognosis was bleak, but Charlie was fighting like a champion. By the time I arrived he had spent many long days and nights in the hospital receiving relentless treatments and fighting for his life. Often the treatment can be brutal, as was the case with Charlie. He looked fatigued and I will admit that I was doubtful that he could overcome such a dire situation.

I slid the rolling doctor's chair close to his bedside and tried to listen intently to what he was saying. It was hard for me to concentrate as I listened because of the medical machines and activity outside of the hospital room. He seemed unwittingly cheerful, in an incredibly positive mood, especially for someone in this state.

As I tried to be fully engaged with what he was saying I noticed a small string tied around his neck. It didn't resemble any medical equipment that I had ever seen before. The front was tied in a bow and I could see the back of the string disappear behind his hospital gown. After a few minutes I got the opportunity to ask him about it. He leaned forward and tugged on the backside of the string revealing a homemade cape made of recycled hospital paraphernalia.

He said, "That's my superhero cape."

I listened as he explained that a very caring doctor had been encouraging him through a series of superhero stories, some stories in which Charlie was the hero, fighting off the evils of the enemy; cancer. This was a doctor that was committed to his healing and knew that it would take strength and a heroic effort to beat this awful disease.

I left humbled. I was focused on an outcome that was not favorable for him, but all Charlie was focused on was winning the war in his body. Charlie beat cancer and devoted his life to helping others do the same by becoming a Pediatric Oncologist.

A few years later I was visiting a child from our church that was bravely battling this horrible disease as a patient of Charlie's. The space was beautiful, hallways marked with bright colors and beautiful displays of encouragement for kids that needed it. Playful music echoed down the halls. Further down the hallway I could see the tail end of what looked like a conga line. As I rounded the corner there was Charlie leading a group of his young patients in a 'flight' exercise through the cancer treatment center.

He was wearing a cape and so was every child in line behind him.

Smiles and laughter interrupted the otherwise scary journey that is cancer. I couldn't help but think back to that moment when Charlie was in a similar battle, but if you were to ask him he would say, "I'm not the hero, *they are.*"

His passion was birthed from a place of despair, as was mine. I knew that I had a hero inside of me, but sometimes I couldn't find my cape. When I suffered the abuse as a young teenager I could have given in to the captivity of pain and never branched out again. When my father rejected me and passed my passion onto my brothers I could have never learned to dream again. When I sat in that Social Security office with my little girls I could have given up on my dream. I could have allowed my passion to die with my dignity.

I chose to never give up.

We enjoyed several great years with lucrative results for us and our franchisees, but it did take a toll on our family. We spent many nights on the phone until 3 a.m. talking to our franchisees and managers through any new endeavor. We worked with our teams on assisting this process. We felt every failure and success our franchisees encountered.

No matter how large our company was we never lost sight of our team being family. I always felt a deep sense of responsibility for our franchisees' success. I prayed for and supported them in every way I knew how. I would forgive payments, repair equipment, and gift essentials to them out of my desire to see them succeed. In a franchise you are only as successful as your weakest link. It takes the entire system to make success for the owners and the company.

With every challenge came a new opportunity to grow and develop. I could have never imagined the fun I would have during this season. Don't get me wrong, it was an exhausting season but there were so many incredible moments.

I remember a time when the CEO of a major national supermarket chain approached one of our shops to assist with their annual company employee appreciation dinner. It was a surge of the usual excitement of a very large catering order. We utilized our learned tactics of developing a precise plan to ensure that the cookies were delivered in the freshest possible timeframe, organized arrivals and goods to prep the product, communicated across multiple teams and executed well. Something that confused us was that this grocery chain is *known* for their baked goods. Why would the CEO choose us to cater their event?

It is important that you honor those that give you the business and thank them for choosing your goods and services above all others in the marketplace. I'm not sure why I always questioned the tremendous blessings that came, but I did, maybe it's humility or awe. Whatever the case might have been—the CEO had chosen us. He later told me it was because of the relationship that he and I had developed during the construction phase of that shop. He came in from time to time and we chatted. It wasn't until the 3rd or 4th visit that I found out that he held the position that he did. I had simply treated him like everyone else that I encountered.

Nonetheless, the order went off without a hitch and we delivered on every promise that we made and exceeded expectations in the places where we could and we gained a lifelong customer in the process.

With multiple operating units, and more interested parties on deck, I found myself at a crossroads. To further spread myself thin or step back and concentrate on some areas that I had neglected, including an appropriate work-life balance. So, the short version is that I chose family.

Kelly and I made the most difficult decision of our lives to date. We sold the business. We negotiated every store, returned the ownership to the franchisees in most cases and moved into a new season for our life and family. I still miss it everyday, years later, and I wouldn't trade the valuable business and life lessons learned in over 10 years of pursuing our Crumby dream. We felt we had left our mark on the industry and our assignment was complete. A question we asked and a question worth asking yourself is, if your business would disappear tomorrow would it be missed?

If there would be one thing that I would encourage every young entrepreneur out there to do it would be this, *if you are ever given a platform, use it.* When you have a small portion of opportunity to have a voice, to create something beautiful, to impact cultural change, do it and remember you have a God-given gift that only you possess. Even when everyone else tells you why it cannot be done, continue your dream and eventually you will land on your success.

So much of winning every battle is being unwilling to give up. Somewhere inside I found the strength to continue my pursuit of that passion which I knew was deep inside of me.

So, march on, brave soldiers, even if the prognosis looks dim and everyone around you is encouraging you to give up. Even if the resources are slim and you are struggling to keep it together. Even if you have some doubts mixing with your faith. In the end you will be a stronger hero for having made the journey.

Success is a subjective and personal concept that can mean different things to different people. We don't have one single shared definition of the word. However, by setting clear goals, developing a personal relationship with Jesus, working hard and being persistent, you can increase your chances of achieving success in your chosen field. Be open to learning and growing, letting God redeem the ups and downs along the way. Success is not a destination, but a journey. With the right mindset and approach, you will shock yourself with what you can achieve.

CHRIS McMURRAY is an author, Pastor, and businessman. He, and his story, have been featured on all major news media outlets on television and radio including Fox News, MSNBC, CNN, iHeartRadio, and more. His innovative business strategies have been utilized in domestic and global companies for more than 15 years. His unique background blends faith and business in a way that challenges and encourages readers to dig deep and find the success that we all strive for. Chris and Kelly live in Orlando, Florida with their two daughters.